$32.50

FUNDRAISING WITH A VISION

A Canvass Guide for Congregations

Edward B. Landreth

Unitarian Universalist Association
Boston

This guide is brought to you in part by your congregation's contribution to the Annual Program Fund.

ISBN 1-55896-355-3

Printed in Canada.

10 9 8 7 6 5 4 3
07 06 05 04

Grateful acknowledgment is made to the many Unitarian Universalists who have led the way to a broader, more abundant sense of stewardship within our denomination. Our movement has been blessed many times over by your work.

Contents

Introduction

This guide is a resource for member congregations of the Unitarian Universalist Association to organize and conduct the annual fundraising needed to support ongoing programs. It outlines the basic annual fundraising process that numerous professional and lay congregation fundraisers have found helpful for many years. Where possible, various options are suggested to accommodate differences in congregations.

The principles in this guide apply to congregations of all sizes, but fundraising techniques are especially directed to small and medium-sized communities (up to 300 persons on average for Sunday attendance). A face-to-face annual canvass at least every other year is recommended to maximize the effectiveness of fundraising along with the other benefits that canvass communication provides for a faith community.

This guide often refers to *The Congregational Handbook*, third edition, which provides assistance with other aspects of church life that affect the ability of a religious community to raise money. Use of *The Congregational Handbook* in conjunction with this guide is strongly encouraged.

Each congregation calls their annual fundraising process by a different name, and some of these are mentioned in Chapter 6 of this book. For consistency, I have used the terms "annual canvass" and "Annual Canvass Committee" throughout. I have also used the word "members" of the congregation in a generic sense that includes members and friends. The word "congregation" is used in place of church, fellowship, society, or other term of reference for Unitarian Universalist organizations.

Although this guide describes only the annual canvass process, congregations raise funds in a variety of ways.

- **The annual canvass** is fundraising that supports the operating budget of the congregation. It consists of an appeal to members and friends for identifiable contributions or pledges of contributions over the congregation's fiscal year.
- **Miscellaneous annual fundraising** includes other fundraising processes that support the annual budget, such as plate collection, fundraising events (bake sales, festivals, rummage sales, service auctions), ongoing sales of particular items (spices, crafts, grocery store scrip), fees from renting out the congregation's space to others, and interest earned on invested funds (endowment, special funds, or operating funds).
- **Special collections** are appeals for a specific purpose, either within the congregation or for an outreach activity outside the annual budget. Examples include a one-time plate collection, a special envelope, and fundraising events.
- **Planned giving** is an ongoing program that encourages members to commit to giving to the congregation at a later time, usually upon death, through bequests and other financial arrangements (see *Congregational Handbook*, Chapter 12).
- **The capital fund drive** is a special fundraising program to raise larger sums of money, usually for building projects (see *Congregational Handbook,* Chapter 13).

Part 1 of this book provides general information about the nature of fundraising. The lay and ministerial leadership of a congregation should use this information to develop their approach for annual fundraising and to assist in recruiting an Annual Canvass Committee.

Money is a subject that for some congregations is difficult to discuss freely as an integral part of spiritual life. However, talking about money can be empowering when it is related to assisting a congregation in reaching its vision and goals. Chapter 1 provides ways of looking at money that may assist in removing some of the barriers and discomfort that accompany this subject.

Many of this guide's process recommendations are explained in Chapter 2. Some people find a face-to-face annual canvass to be difficult, even burdensome. However, the canvass process is not only most effective for fundraising but builds community, provides a ministry, and is fun.

The rest of this guide provides the Annual Canvass Committee with specific assistance in organizing and conducting an annual fund drive for the congregation. Part 2 covers the basics of organizing and conducting an annual canvass throughout a church, including options for congregations who don't want to hold an annual canvass. Part 3 is an orientation for canvass volunteers and includes handy tips.

In some instances, information provided on American tax laws is not suitable for Canadian congregations. I recommend that you contact the Canadian Unitarian Council, 55 Eglinton Avenue East, Suite 705, Toronto, ONT M4P 1G8, Canada, telephone (416) 489-4121, for answers to Canadian tax law questions.

"Giving Voice to Our Vision" is a 14-minute video designed to accompany this guide. The video features members of Unitarian Universalist congregations expressing their feelings about the canvassing process, thus providing an emotional viewpoint that the printed page of this guide cannot convey effectively. "Giving Voice to Our Vision" (Item #7001) is available from the UUA Bookstore for $12.00. To order, call toll-free 1-800-215-9076.

PART ONE

The Nature of Fundraising

1. Talking About Money

Many congregations find it difficult to talk about money. They view it as "a necessary evil" rather than an opportunity to help the congregation achieve its vision. The financial health of a congregation is usually indicated by the way it talks (or avoids talking) about money.

It's ironic that many people have problems discussing a subject that is a necessary ingredient of daily living. Obtaining food, fuel, clothing, and maintenance requires the use of money. In the barter system that preceded money, goods and services had a value expressed only in relationship to each other. Those who did not know the relative values of the items bartered were at a disadvantage in a transaction. Concern for the inequity in barter transactions was one of the significant motivations that led to the use of precious metals as a common substance, called money. In addition to convenience, money provides a relative value on all goods and services that results in transactions that are more fair to the participants. Thus, the origins of money were rooted in some of the qualities that we profess in our religious life.

As the system of trade goods and services developed through history, the subject of money gained negative connotations. Some factors leading to these negative perceptions include:

- unwise exertion of power resulting from the accumulation of money
- love of money for itself rather than for the good it can do
- equating the worth of a person to the amount of money that person has or earns.

Talking about one's own money is considered bad form. How often are children admonished not to speak about family finances outside the home? As a consequence of these negative aspects, people are uncomfortable discussing money, especially in a religious environment. These negative perceptions do not seem congruent with the religious values we profess.

Our congregations need money as much as any other person, group, or organization to exist and to flourish. Money is one of the many gifts that members need to provide to realize the congregation's shared vision. If negative perceptions of money are allowed to get in the way of a congregation addressing its money issues, the life of the congregation is continually hampered by a shortage of resources.

How do congregations perpetuate the discomfort in talking about money? Here are some observations.

- *Money is discussed only once a year at annual canvass time.* The rest of the year, the subject is not raised so members and friends don't have to be bothered about it. Thus talking about money is equated only with asking for money, not with any aspect of using the money to further the vision of the congregation.
- *Money is discussed only in terms of meeting a congregation's budget or monetary goal.* Instead of relating money as a warm connection that can unite a congregation to accomplish its vision and mission, it is viewed as an impersonal table of specific expenses, just numbers on a spreadsheet.
- *The amount of money any individual contributes is kept an absolute secret from everyone in the congregation.* Many Unitarian Universalist congregations recognize and honor people who give their time and talents, but not their money. Even canvassers are not allowed to know what their prospects contributed in previous years. In one sense, an individual's money contribution represents a time contribution, the time spent earning that money, yet we have difficulty acknowledging this form of gift.
- *The budget is developed by the financial leadership and presented to the congregation for approval.* The congregation has little or no input into the priorities that need to be considered when developing its budget. The congregation only sees a completed statement of expected income and expenses and does not sense the potentials that the budget is planned to assist. In some congregations, the leadership creates and approves the budget with no involvement by other members of the congregation.
- *Money is discussed in terms of the congregation's needs rather than what*

contributions can do to help the congregation move toward its vision and goals. To many people this may be a subtle point, but it can be a powerful subconscious influence in the attitude of the congregation toward money and the annual canvass. Instead of viewing money and generous giving as positive tools for achieving congregation goals and vision, does your congregation fret over expenses, fearing that each expenditure uses a scarce resource? The unspoken, underlying assumption here is that of scarcity rather than that of generosity.

Thinking about these behaviors and the other factors that influence our ideas about money, we can change the way we talk about it to put it into a positive light. Congregations need money to support programs that will reach toward their goals and vision. Thus, conversations about money need to be in that vein: What it can do for the congregation. This is true empowerment, the use of money along with all the other gifts of its members to enhance the spirituality of the congregation.

Here are some guidelines about money talk.

- Money matters are a year-round open conversation in the congregation, becoming as natural as ordinary money transactions in our daily lives.
- Money conversations are informative when they relate to how the congregation will move toward its vision, goals, and aspirations.
- Money discussions are empowering for the congregation when they center on its priorities for the future.
- Money talk is inspirational when we assume a generosity of giving rather than a scarcity of income.

Talking about money means using several communication vehicles within the congregation—the newsletter, the Sunday Order of Service, announcements, sermon topics, committee discussions, posters, bulletin boards, etc. —along with all the other information communicated within the congregation. Communicating in this way, money talk becomes a part of the everyday conversation, as in the secular world. It becomes a part of our religious or spiritual life rather than an adjunct that is only tolerated because it is needed.

Talking about money in terms of how it will help us move into the future will blunt the complaint, "They are always talking about money." This complaint is heard when the conversation is about *need* instead of the *vision* or *mission* of the congregation. When talking only about needs and the dollars and cents of individual expenditures, the subject appears to focus on money, which can be boring and irritating over time. When conversation is framed about vision and goals, and what funds are needed to achieve them, money has a spiritual meaning in terms of the life of the congregation.

2. Why Do We Canvass?

People give money because they are asked! No fundraising effort is successful without asking for contributions. The annual canvass process described in this section is based on a careful manner of asking members for contribution pledges within a community-building visit.

Consider the motivations of people who are asked to contribute money to their Unitarian Universalist congregation. If you asked them why they give, you might get a list similar to the following:

- gratitude for our liberal religious faith
- satisfaction with the religious community
- interest in helping others in the congregation
- commitment to the congregation's vision or mission
- pride of association
- gratitude for the ministry
- helping others in the larger community
- living Unitarian Universalist values
- contributions will make a difference
- returning gifts already received
- investment in the future.

Note that all these motivations for giving are emotional or from the heart. *Contributions come from the heart, not the head.* People decide to give based on their perceived emotional attachment or commitment to the congregation and to Unitarian Universalism and on how that commitment triggers one or more of these motivations.

The fundraising process in this guide emphasizes the positive motivations for giving. Guilt is a powerful motivation but a negative one that is often used in fundraising, even in churches. Unitarian Universalist congregations are encouraged to avoid its use. Guilt and other negative motivations often leave some bad feelings, especially after contributions are made. It may also lead to a higher number of pledges that are not honored. By using positive motivations, all parties will be satisfied with the process before, during, and after the annual canvass.

The strength of any fundraising campaign rests on triggering these positive emotions within potential contributors. The keys to accomplishing this are to share the vision, relate programs and activities to that vision, and deepen the sense of commitment.

Sharing the Vision

Each active member of a congregation, whether he or she realizes it, carries some vision of what he or she would like the congregation to be in the future. These visions vary, from keeping things the same to different scenarios of change. The vision each person holds influences his or her motivations and actions as he or she relates to the congregation.

A congregation that develops a shared vision through dialogue among its members gains a focus. A shared vision empowers congregation members to agree on a direction and to move toward that common goal. For more information on how to develop vision and mission statements, see Chapter 2 in *The Congregational Handbook*.

A congregation's shared vision strengthens its annual fundraising process. Congregations that lack a shared vision have a more difficult time developing a spark in their fundraising. This lack of vision makes it difficult to articulate why members should contribute generously. Having a shared vision provides the answer to the question, "Why are we doing this?" It provides the emotional reason for contributing to a congregation's annual canvass.

Relating to the Vision

When presenting information to members about budget and finances, a congregation is encouraged to follow the mission budget process described in Chapter 12 of *The Congregational Handbook*. Relating the budget to a congregation's vision and mission provides a link between the financial and the emotional. It also answers the question, "Why are we doing this?"

During an annual canvass it helps to remind members that programs and activities supported by their contributions also support the congregation's shared vision and mission. An annual canvass drive that successfully communicates these relationships will be most effective. The emphasis should not be on how much programs and activities cost, but on how contributions support these programs and activities to further the congregation and Unitarian Universalism.

Communications that relate programs and activities to a shared vision should take place in the months preceding an actual canvass. This advance information prepares members so that when they are asked for pledges, they know what the annual canvass is for and why, and have made a decision to contribute. More than the knowledge, members *feel* the connection between what they are asked to contribute and the vision their money supports.

Deepening the Sense of Commitment

Pledges to an annual canvass are largely based on two factors: the *capability* of the individual to give and the *commitment* of that individual to the congregation. The annual canvass process cannot influence the capability of a member to contribute; however, the process can influence the individual's *feelings* of commitment. Often individuals don't realize the degree of their commitment until they have the opportunity to talk about it. It's like many other emotions and feelings that are not realized to their full extent until they become articulated through dialogue, prayer and meditation, or other means.

A face-to-face request for a pledge to the annual canvass provides an opportunity for dialogue to take place about commitment. You can start a canvass visit with an open-ended question that stimulates thoughts about the congregation, such as, "What has happened in our congregation this past year that is most important to you?" or, "What aspect of this faith community has the most meaning for you at this stage in your life?" The specific question is not as important as the discussion that follows. The discussion may lead in any of many different paths, each equally valuable in building community.

Some canvass visits may be a sharing of experiences between the canvasser and the contributor. Other visits may be a means of answering questions or providing information. Some may result in hearing concerns or complaints. Whatever form it takes, a canvass visit should allow people to express their feelings about the congregation. It needs to let conversation happen so members can discuss matters that otherwise would remain unspoken. This type of conversation should take up most of the time in a canvass visit.

Only toward the end of a canvass visit should the subject of a pledge be raised. At this point, a canvasser may answer questions about the congregation's budget or finances. The canvasser asks for a pledge; the pledge card is signed; thanks are given; and the visit is completed.

What really takes place during a canvass call? The canvass call provides a number of important benefits, not only to the annual canvass, but also to the congregation in other ways.

- **Deepening commitment.** The potential contributor expresses feelings about the congregation, thus gaining a better sense of commitment.
- **Building community.** The canvasser and potential contributor get to know each other better than before the call. The call is a great opportunity for canvassers to get to know more people in the congregation.
- **Performing a ministry.** The components of the canvass call—communicating, listening, affirming, informing, caring, etc.—are characteristics of ministering. When else during the year do we have the opportunity to call on a congregation's membership?
- **Having fun.** This may seem surprising, but isn't it fun to get to know new people or other people better, to have some time just to talk about the congregation that is so important in our lives, to feel that it is performing an important ministry? Why should canvassing be a chore, considering all the positive benefits it provides? What is the congregation but a community where contact between and among members is beneficial to all concerned, a fun process?

Ask any fundraising professional and he or she will tell you that the best way to get a generous contribution is to ask for it at the end of a face-to-face canvass visit. Some of the issues that hold people back from canvassing are:

- we are tired of canvassing
- we cannot recruit enough canvassers
- people do not have the time for a canvass call in these times
- members do not like to ask for money
- members will not allow canvassers into their homes.

We are tired of canvassing. This statement usually occurs after canvasses that focus only on asking for pledges. Canvasses can be much more than that. They involve important dialogue between the canvasser and potential contributor about the congregation, which builds community and performs a ministry. The process of talking with other Unitarian Universalists about our faith community is fun, and people do not tire of it.

We cannot recruit enough canvassers. It is difficult to recruit canvassers if potential recruits perceive the following:

- a poorly organized Annual Canvass Committee
- recruiting just before the canvass period
- a half-hearted recruitment
- poorly managed previous canvass
- canvass considered a drudgery, no fun
- canvass considered just asking for money
- canvassers aren't treated respectfully by the congregation.

A well-organized Annual Canvass Committee starts its communication process months before the annual canvass, emphasizing the community-building, ministry, and fun aspects of the canvass along with a message of canvassing for a vision. If members look forward to the canvass visit, if canvassers are part of an energized canvass team, and if the committee recruits canvassers enthusiastically, it will be easy to find members willing to canvass.

People do not have the time for a canvass call in these times. Active members of any congregation are always busy people, whether involved in outside activities or projects in the home. The willingness to participate in a canvass visit is a matter of priorities. If members *feel* the canvass call is important for reasons other than just asking for a pledge, they will set aside time to welcome a canvasser. The congregation has to make the canvass visit an important part of its spiritual life in moving toward its shared vision, not just a tolerated means to raise money to pay the bills.

Members do not like to ask for money. A canvass visit results in a pledge after a dialogue that shares values. After talking about the vision and goals of the congregation, it is a natural progression to ask for support for the community we share. There is no pressure, belittlement, or negative tone associated with asking for a pledge that would result in bad feelings then or later. Furthermore, members who accept a canvass visit expect to be asked. The goal is for both the canvasser and the contributor to feel good about the entire process.

Members will not allow canvassers into their homes. You can alert members about annual canvass visits by mentioning them in annual canvass communications. Let members know what a canvass visit is like, emphasizing that it can be as informal as sitting across the kitchen table with coffee or that it can be held in locations other than the home. If someone is uncomfortable with a canvass visit in his or her home, the canvasser can arrange a meeting in a coffee shop or at the church in a quiet room. The canvasser can even invite the member to his or her home. The important thing is the opportunity for *dialogue,* whenever and wherever it might take place.

The culture of a congregation determines its attitude toward canvassing. If there is difficulty in canvassing, there are ways to modify this attitude with good organization, communication, and a view that the annual canvass is not about raising money, but about reaching a vision or dream. Attitudes do not change overnight; however, they can change. Many congregations embrace canvassing as a significant process in its life each year and gain benefits from the process.

PART TWO

Annual Canvass Basics

3. Creating an Annual Canvass Committee

The Annual Canvass Committee oversees the development and implementation of the annual canvass process. This committee is very important to the life of the congregation so its composition cannot be taken lightly. The committee chair and members should be individuals who want to contribute their talents and skills in helping the congregation achieve its vision and goals. It is important for the governing board of the congregation to see that qualified members of the congregation be recruited for this committee.

The Annual Canvass Committee has several functions to perform during the year's fundraising process. The following pages outline the tasks and skills required for each component of this committee. In smaller congregations, some committee members might serve multiple functions, or specific functions may be divided and combined with others. In larger congregations, each function might need the attention of an individual or a small team. All the functions outlined in this chapter apply to congregations of all sizes.

Two persons who are encouraged to become a part of the Annual Canvass Committee are the minister and the board president. The minister is especially important to an annual canvass. By participating in the canvass process, he or she sends the message that it is okay to discuss money within the spiritual dimension of the congregation's life. His or her participation also underlines the importance of the annual canvass in the yearly flow of congregational activities.

In addition to the committee chair, some congregations elect or appoint an associate chair of the Annual Canvass Committee. Often it is understood that the associate chair will serve as the chair the following year, in effect spending a year as an understudy.

Organizational Chart

- Annual Canvass Chair or Co-chairs
  - Associate Chair
  - Advance Gifts Chair
    - Canvassers (up to 6)
  - General Canvass Chair
    - Canvasser Team Leader (up to 8)
      - Canvassers (4 to 7)
    - Canvasser Team Leader
      - Canvassers
    - Canvasser Team Leader
      - Canvassers
  - Annual Canvass Administrator
  - Annual Canvass Treasurer
  - Canvass Kickoff Chair
  - Communications Chair
  - Continuing Canvass/Follow-up Chair

Annual Canvass Chair

The Annual Canvass Chair is responsible for the overall direction of the annual canvass drive, from the initial planning stages until the final report is submitted to the leadership of the congregation.

The chair is responsible for overseeing the recruitment of the Annual Canvass Committee and chairs all the meetings of that group. He or she represents the canvass at congregational events and at training events for other annual canvass team members. He or she speaks for the annual canvass team.

The Annual Canvass Chair leads the committee to finalize the annual canvass plan and calendar and coordinates them with the church's master calendar. Additionally, the chair is responsible for the committee's implementation of the annual canvass plan and calendar, ensuring that the tasks and events take place as agreed upon by the committee.

This position is essentially a top management job and requires someone who can motivate others, delegate authority, and collaborate with other annual canvass volunteers in decision making. Above all, this person must be fully committed to the success of the annual canvass and the health, growth, and progress of the church. An annual canvass is a major opportunity for all members and friends of the congregation to renew their individual commitment to it and to one another. The Annual Canvass Chair is the layperson who leads this formal renewal of a covenant, which is one of the essentials of a healthy congregation.

The Annual Canvass Chair can expect to spend one to three hours in weekly or biweekly meetings during the canvass, and may spend an additional two to four hours a week making phone calls and preparing for meetings. During the remainder of the active congregation year, he or she can expect to spend five to ten hours per month in meetings and phone conversations.

This position can be shared by two people acting as co-chairs, provided each person understands which portions of the overall activity are under his or her control, and for which he or she is responsible. Clear communication between co-chairs is essential for this leadership model to be effective.

Advance Gifts Chair

The Advance Gifts Chair leads a small team of up to six selected canvassers who will be seeking commitments of support from members most able to make generous pledges. This team will seek pledges in advance of the general annual canvass to form the core support for the annual canvass and give it momentum. These types of pledges need to be obtained early so canvass leadership can evaluate the potential for success and determine if additional, special efforts are needed to reach the overall goal of the annual canvass. The advance gifts canvassed by this team will likely account for one-half or more of the total pledge for the entire canvass.

The Advance Gifts Chair must be willing and able to make a major personal pledge, for this is one area where leadership by example is critical. Like the Annual Canvass Chair, it is essential that this person be fully committed to the goals and success of the annual canvass.

Advance and Special Gifts pledges are sought from:

- all people on the annual canvass team
- current major pledges (most likely the top 20 percent)
- the congregational leadership
- enthusiastic new members who seem able to make such a commitment.

The Advance Gifts Chair oversees the training and preparation of team members and also participates as a leader and canvasser. He or she is responsible for recruiting additional canvassers from among members who will be asked for an advance gift, providing these additional canvassers with the canvass plan and calendar, ensuring that they attend the workshop sessions for canvassers, and assigning pledge cards for this phase of the canvass. Workshops are coordinated with the Annual Canvass Chair(s).

The chair coordinates with the Canvass Kickoff Chair to plan an advance gift event that launches this part of the canvass. He or she can anticipate spending two to four hours weekly or biweekly in committee meetings during the annual canvass, and an additional two to three hours a week during the weeks before and during the Advance Gifts phase to recruit canvassers and help train them.

General Canvass Chair

The General Canvass Chair's responsibilities include recruiting, training, and supporting the annual canvass teams and canvassers for the general canvass. Much of this activity, especially the recruitment and training aspects, is coordinated with the Advance Gifts Chair. The General Canvass Chair also oversees assigning pledge cards to canvassers for this phase of the canvass. Like the Annual Canvass Chair, it is essential that this person be fully committed to the goals and success of the annual canvass.

This position requires someone with good organizational skills as well as the ability to recruit, motivate, and manage people—and to help them overcome any hesitancy about canvassing. He or she will organize the canvassers into teams of four to seven canvassers, each led by a canvasser team leader. This team approach improves communication flow between the Annual Canvass Committee and the canvassers. It is important that this person be prepared to maintain close communications with and support the canvasser team leaders and ultimately the canvassers during the general annual canvass drive.

The General Canvass Chair, working closely with the Annual Canvass Administrator, keeps a master list of who is working in the annual canvass organization and to whom each pledge card has been assigned. Canvasser team leaders are responsible for reporting each signed pledge card so that accurate, up-to-date reports are available to the Annual Canvass Committee.

The General Canvass Chair can anticipate spending two to four hours weekly or biweekly in committee meetings during the canvass, and an additional two to three hours a week during the weeks before and during the general canvass to recruit canvassers and help train them. During the general canvass itself, this position may require two to three hours a day keeping in touch with canvassers to assess the progress of the annual canvass and supporting their efforts.

Annual Canvass Administrator

The Annual Canvass Administrator is responsible for developing a list of potential contributors to be canvassed during the annual canvass, sending appeal letters to members who cannot be canvassed personally because of distance, and keeping the minutes and calendar of the Annual Canvass Committee.

He or she will work with the Membership Committee and/or the congregation's office to develop a list of potential contributors, including members, long-term friends, new friends recently attending worship, and any others who might support the programs of the congregation. This data will be given to the Annual Canvass Treasurer.

The administrator will work with the Communications Chair to write letters to members and friends who cannot be canvassed directly—those who live out of town and those who cannot receive visitors. He or she will see that minutes of each Annual Canvass Committee meeting are written and promptly sent to each committee member. Included will be an updated calendar with all annual canvass activities and responsible individuals identified.

This position requires someone with an attention to detail and the ability to write well.

Annual Canvass Treasurer

The Annual Canvass Treasurer is responsible for setting up and maintaining the data input and retrieval systems needed to keep the Annual Canvass Committee well informed about the canvass progress, pledges returned and filed, outstanding pledge cards, etc.

He or she should be involved in designing or obtaining pledge cards, assuring that the information needed for accurate reports and analysis will be available. He or she also provides reports of pledging activity to the Annual Canvass Committee as requested and distributes a final report, including pledging projections, to the congregation's board.

The Annual Canvass Treasurer works during the annual canvass and continues working with the Follow-up Committee, which includes sending thank-you and confirmation letters, record-keeping, adjusting unpaid or overdue pledges, etc.

This position requires someone with the ability to create and keep accurate financial records and reports, and a good knowledge of computer spreadsheet programs. Having information on the tax implications of charitable gifts may be helpful. He or she can expect to spend two to four hours per week in committee meetings and an additional one to three hours weekly before the Advance Gifts Canvass to set up record-keeping systems and through the remainder of the canvass. Once the final report is completed, he or she will spend one to three hours monthly or quarterly assisting in the preparation of statements and reports to the board.

Canvass Kickoff Chair

The Canvass Kickoff Chair coordinates all activities needed to ensure the success and maximum possible attendance at all annual canvass social events, including the kickoff event and the advance gifts event. He or she also recruits other members of the Canvass Kickoff Team as required.

This team is responsible for the following tasks:

- Securing sites, setting menus and styles of service, and making table arrangements for events. Coordinates with Communications Committee to prepare and mail invitations.
- Recruiting hosts to address invitations, call to confirm acceptance, and welcome those invited to their tables at events. The hosts should not be canvassers.
- Arranging for entertainment at events, coordinating with the Communications Chair so that the program flows smoothly and ends on time.

The person for this position needs to have good organizational abilities and be able to deal well with details, delegate authority, and have a knack for dreaming up and putting on good, fun parties! He or she can spend two to four hours in weekly or biweekly meetings of the Annual Canvass Committee as well as two to three hours a week with his or her own team. The time commitment may increase during the week or two before events.

It is strongly recommended that a congregational fellowship event be planned that does not call upon members of the congregation to prepare and serve food or otherwise work during the event!

Communications Chair

The Communications Chair is responsible for the canvass communication that will create enthusiasm for the annual canvass and motivate members to give generously. This person will recruit two to three other members of the Communications Team that will include artistic, writing, and creative talent.

The Communications Chair is a key member of the Annual Canvass Committee and is responsible for helping the committee develop the canvass's theme and logo, for leading the Communications Team in developing a communication plan, and for producing various canvass communications.

The Communications Team will prepare a variety of annual canvass messages to be repeated several times and in various ways that respond to different learning styles: visual (images), auditory (sounds, spoken words), and kinesthetic (feeling, action).

Examples of communication media within the congregation include:

- posters, cards, and signs in the congregation's building
- letters to the congregation from the Annual Canvass Committee, minister, and governing board
- canvass brochure
- invitations to the kickoff event
- articles in the congregation's newsletter
- special information sheets enclosed in newsletters
- announcements at Sunday worship services.

The person for this position needs to be open to creative ideas and have some organizational skills and attention to detail. In recruiting other members of the team, he or she can round out the team's skills. The time commitment for this position is two to four hours per week. During the planning phase, an additional one to two hours per week may be required.

Continuing Canvass/Follow-up Chair

After the annual canvass has been completed, the Continuing Canvass/ Follow-up Chair leads a team of three to seven people to do the following:

- Complete the canvassing of those not able to be contacted during the annual canvass. This brings closure to the annual canvass.
- Monitor the ongoing receipt of pledges and contact those who fall behind in their pledges. This is an important outreach to those who might be otherwise lost as members of the congregation.
- Visit and solicit pledges from new members. New members will become the backbone of the congregation in later years; encouraging them to pledge generously from the beginning of their association is important.
- Promote other forms of giving. Keep the congregation informed about further giving options by holding workshops on planned giving, bequests, etc., and visit those who may wish to make special gifts.
- Advise next year's Annual Canvass Committee. The continuing canvass is part of the year-round canvass process and provides the bridge from one annual canvass to the next.

These functions are often neglected, but they can make a huge difference in the success of a canvass. The chair of this team should know fundraising techniques and have a clear commitment to the congregation's financial well-being. Also, he or she should be able to work well with people in difficult and awkward situations. The time commitment required is normally one to two hours a week and extends throughout the year following the canvass.

The Annual Canvass Committee should meet at least once a month during the congregation's year. During the initial planning phase, the month preceding, and the month of the canvass, the committee might want to meet more often. Each meeting should have an agenda, preferably distributed a few days before the meeting. A recording secretary should be appointed (possibly the annual canvass administrator) to document all significant activity status and decisions made. These minutes need to be completed and distributed to committee members and other congregation leadership as needed within a few days of the meeting. This ensures that everyone is reminded of what has happened and what needs to happen in the committee's life.

4. The Annual Canvass Calendar

Creating an annual canvass calendar puts the fundraising process into perspective within your congregation. The following calendar shows the major elements of an annual canvass throughout the year. (Also see Appendix 5: Sample Canvass Calendar.)

The annual canvass process is a year-round effort. An Annual Canvass Committee that is actively committed during the entire year reduces the peak workloads and stress that volunteers experience when the process is condensed into a few months' effort. Having a year-round effort allows for good planning, time to do the tasks well, and for some of the fun and social benefits that a well-run committee experiences instead of the stress of severe time constraints. Over time, it may be easier to recruit Annual Canvass Committee members when the year-round process is perceived as a more manageable pace than the panic and high workload of a few month's effort.

As described in Chapter 2, communication throughout the year is an important element in an effective annual canvass process. Shortening the annual canvass activity from a year-round process usually means reducing the amount and quality of communications between the congregation and its members, which reduces the effectiveness of the message.

The elements of an annual canvass calendar are the same whether the canvass is held in the spring or the fall. However, when planning for a fall canvass, summer months have to be considered. If the congregation is relatively inactive during the summer, those months should be excluded from the schedule. If the church has some activity and communication during the summer months, that fact needs to be considered in planning the overall schedule.

The calendar, once created, is a good management tool for the Annual Canvass Committee to track all activities during the year. Updating the calendar with details and responsibility assignments at each committee meeting and providing a copy to each member is an ideal means of committee communication.

Annual Canvass Calendar

Month 1 *Planning* (Second month after last canvass)	Annual Canvass Committee organizes. Recruit full committee. Plan annual canvass. Make schedule. Choose theme. Communication Committee organizes.
Month 2 *Plan communications*	Communication Committee develops communication plan. Annual Canvass Committee meets. Review communication plan. Refine schedule.
Month 3 *Start communications*	Annual Canvass Committee reviews schedules. Communications development starts. Newsletter articles start. Kickoff Committee organizes.
Month 4 *Plan kickoff*	Annual Canvass Committee reviews schedules. Communications continue. Start brochure development. Kickoff planning starts.

Month 5 *Recruit canvassers*	Annual Canvass Committee reviews schedules. Start canvasser recruitment. Communications continue.
Month 6 *Communicate*	Annual Canvass Committee reviews schedules. Communications move into high gear.
Month 7 *Communicate*	Annual Canvass Committee reviews schedules. Communications continue. Budget discussions start.
Month 8 *Create brochure*	Annual Canvass Committee reviews schedules. Brochure completed. Budget discussions are ongoing.
Month 9 *Recruit canvassers*	Annual Canvass Committee reviews schedules. Prepare canvasser kits. Complete canvasser recruitment. Preliminary budget adopted, canvass goals set. Brochure printed and mailed to congregation. Advance Gift Canvasser Workshop held.

Month 10 *Advance gifts made*	Annual Canvass Committee reviews schedules. Advance gift event held. Advance Gift Canvass starts (generally lasts one or two weeks). Advance Gift Canvass ends (generally one to two weeks before general canvass). Canvasser assignments completed (required for canvasser workshop). Canvasser Workshop(s) (generally within two weeks of the canvass). Advance Gift results available.
Month 11 *General canvass begins*	Canvass kickoff (generally during weekend at the start of the annual canvass). Start of General Canvass (generally lasts two weeks). Completion of General Canvass. Cleanup of remaining calls. Announce results to congregation.
Month 12 *Follow-up*	Celebration event for Annual Canvass Committee and Canvassers. Evaluation of annual canvass process for the year. (What went well, what could be improved, and how?) Follow-up team created. Canvass new members and friends (continuing activity). Recruit leadership and nucleus of next year's Annual Canvass Committee.

5. Planning

The first major task of an Annual Canvass Committee is to plan the year's annual canvass effort. The end product of the planning will be a theme for the annual canvass and a detailed schedule of events. It is very important that the minister and chair of the governing board be part of the planning process because the annual canvass is a significant event in the congregation's life and must be integrated into the congregation's calendar of activities.

Schedule

To schedule the annual canvass, consult the congregation's calendar of events. First, determine when the actual annual canvass will take place. Most congregations allow two weeks for an active canvass period, the length depending on circumstances within the congregation. Also schedule the canvass kickoff event; many congregations like that event to take place during the beginning weekend of the canvass. Please note that the period between mid-November and early January is a difficult time for fundraising because of the holidays. It is also best not to schedule the annual canvass during a period when another major congregational activity that requires large time commitments is scheduled.

Second, working backward from the dates of the annual canvass, schedule the following dates using Appendix 5: Sample Canvass Calendar as a guide:

- canvasser workshop(s) for the annual canvass
- beginning and end of advance gift canvass
- canvasser workshop for the advance gift canvass
- canvasser recruitment completed.

Third, working backward from the dates established, estimate the length of time to complete tasks and plan beginning and intermediate dates for the following activities, being careful not to underestimate the times involved. Along with the dates, note the names of people who will be responsible and directly involved:

- recruit canvassers
- plan and organize the canvass kickoff event
- develop a database of potential contributors
- assign canvassers to potential contributors
- plan the canvasser workshop(s).

Fourth, identify the key times that information should be conveyed to the congregation about the annual canvass process. This will be a preliminary list; the Communications Committee should develop a more comprehensive communications plan for the Annual Canvass Committee to review and approve. This step provides the Communications Committee with initial guidelines.

The decisions made during this initial planning session, as with all the Annual Canvass Committee meetings, should be documented in the minutes. The dates should be put in a calendar format for the convenience of the committee members. The calendar will become the focus for reviewing the progress of the annual canvass process in subsequent committee meetings.

Theme

The theme for the annual canvass needs to be established by the Annual Canvass Committee. The theme should relate to the vision or mission focus of the following year's budget (see Chapter 12 in *The Congregational Handbook)*. If a shared vision or mission focus has not been developed, the theme should relate to the perceived direction toward which the congregation is headed or a positive program or initiative within the congregation.

The purpose of a theme is to provide congregation members with a constant reminder of why the annual canvass is being held. When the theme accompanies communications material, it catches the eye or ear and provides a recognition factor. It also separates annual canvass communications from other forms of communication within the congregation.

The theme should be simple—a few catchy words or a *very* short statement is most effective. Otherwise, it loses its ability to be easily recognized. Some annual canvass themes that have been used by other congregations include the following:

- "Canvass of Dreams"
  —Unitarian Universalist Fellowship of Gainesville, Florida
- "Giving to Grow"
  —Unitarian Universalist Church of Palo Alto, California
- "Living in Harmoney"
  —First Unitarian Universalist Church of Columbus, Ohio
- "To Care and Share"
  —First Parish Church United, Westford, Massachusetts
- "Shaping the New World"
  —First Parish in Cambridge, Massachusetts
- "Reach for the Stars"
  —Bay Area Unitarian Universalist Fellowship, Houston, Texas
- "Building On Our Past—Sailing Toward Our Future"
  —First Parish in Plymouth, Massachusetts

To develop a theme, a brainstorming exercise is helpful. Each member of the committee suggests one or more themes; someone notes each one on paper, visible to the group. Members are encouraged to build on these suggestions. When ideas are exhausted, the group should discuss the themes listed, commenting on likes, dislikes, and other reactions to words, phrases, and ideas. Often through this discussion certain existing suggestions or new ones crafted from the comments will appeal to the group. If at this session no clear theme seems to be most favored, postpone further discussion until the next meeting. With all the ideas recorded in the minutes, members can consider them before the next meeting. Taking advantage of this subconscious processing of ideas, "sleeping on it," can result in a stronger theme statement.

In addition to a theme that is expressed in a slogan, a logo, which is a small drawing, symbol, or other visual representation of the idea embodied in the theme, is a powerful visual symbol for the annual canvass. This logo, used with the theme, provides an even greater recognition factor to annual canvass communications. A logo should help members make the emotional connection between the congregation's vision and the annual canvass. Its basic idea can be envisioned by the Annual Canvass Committee with the detailed design made by the Communications Committee.

Canvass Alternatives

Fundraising wisdom states that a face-to-face canvass visit leads to the most successful drives. However, some congregations wish to vary their fundraising process from year to year, or to take a break from recruiting canvassers. Congregations should not stay away from a face-to-face canvass for more than two years.

Taking a vacation from the face-to-face canvass process does not mean giving up the other important aspects of fundraising, such as the year-round Annual Canvass Committee and a communication process. Communications is even more important in an alternative canvass because fewer members will be approached directly during pledging.

Here are some alternatives to an annual canvass.

- ***Congregational dinner.*** A congregational dinner is organized where pledge cards are distributed, filled out, and turned in. Often a member of the Annual Canvass Committee is seated at each table to distribute cards, answer questions, and collect completed cards. There may be a program tuned to the fundraising theme.

  This approach reaches only those members who attend the dinner. A well-organized follow-up telephone campaign needs to be initiated after the event to reach members who were not present. After each telephone call that results in a pledge decision, a pledge card with a self-addressed, stamped envelope needs to be sent along with a "thank you." Returned cards need to be monitored closely and follow-up calls need to be made to people not returning cards. To reduce the calling load, others outside the Annual Canvass Committee need to be recruited.

- ***Sunday worship.*** Similar to the congregational dinner, pledge cards are distributed at Sunday worship and collected by ushers after completion.

Often the sermon or worship program may focus on the mission budget to build commitment. Again, a well-organized follow-up telephone campaign needs to be in place to obtain pledges from congregation members who are not present.

- ***Mail solicitation.*** This process involves sending pledge cards and return envelopes to every member. After a period of time, a follow-up letter should be sent to members who have not responded. After that, a follow-up telephone campaign needs to be initiated.
- ***Telephone solicitation.*** In this alternative, the entire pledge solicitation is done by telephone. Solicitors can be given scripts to assist them in making the opening of the call and asking for a pledge. Many congregations obtain the use of a facility with several telephones and schedule one or more evening phonathons, making the event a social occasion by furnishing a meal or refreshments to the telephone solicitors. Having the solicitors work in one place provides mutual support and enjoyment in the process. To people who pledge over the telephone, a pledge card and stamped, addressed envelope along with a "thank you" are sent immediately following the call.

In each of these alternatives, a well-organized follow-up is required. If personal visits are involved, it is important that you do not convey the message, "if you don't send in your pledge card, we'll call on you," using the personal visit as a threat rather than the fun process it is. For more information about face-to-face canvassing, see Chapter 11.

Communication is the backbone of any method for collecting pledges. Each member needs to be well informed about any fundraising efforts before being asked for a pledge. For more information about communicating with the congregation, see Chapter 6.

For an effective fundraising effort using an alternative to the canvass, all the other elements of the process described in this guide need to be present.

6. Communications

Communications are the backbone of an annual canvass. To effectively raise money, a congregation needs to motivate its members to give by letting them know that the canvass is needed to realize its vision and achieve its mission. This message must be broadcast before the annual canvass, when members are forming decisions about their pledges

Throughout the annual canvass cycle, it is also important to keep the congregation informed of the canvass's progress. Information about who is involved on various canvass teams and what they are doing makes the canvass process more visible. During and after the canvass period, update the congregation on the progress of the number of pledges and the total pledge amount. Some congregations create a list of members who have pledged and update it weekly, on a poster or in the congregation newsletter, as a public acknowledgment of contributions. This level of communication emphasizes the human side of the annual canvass.

What to Call Your Annual Canvass

The annual fundraising process in your congregation can be called a number of ways, such as the Annual Fund Drive, Annual Fund Campaign, Annual Canvass, or Every Member Canvass. An advance gift canvass could also be called a leadership gift canvass or leadership canvass.

There are more special names within your congregation, possibly one that reflects your faith community. Such a name will give your annual fundraising process a more personal face. Some congregations develop a new name each year, usually tying it to the mission emphasis for that year.

The Communications Plan

The Communications Team should become active as soon as the Annual Canvass Committee develops a schedule and theme for the annual canvass. Taking the theme and the Committee's recommendations of key communications milestones, the Communications Team should develop a plan that shows the dates when all communications will be available and the intermediate milestones in developing each of the communications, including who is responsible for each activity. This communications plan becomes a part of the Annual Canvass Committee schedule, to be reviewed at each of the committee's meetings.

Communication Content

Communication should be motivational and informational. It needs to articulate a congregation's vision and mission, what actions are being taken to move toward this vision and mission, and how the annual canvass will enable you to take these actions. It should also inform people how the canvass will be conducted, why canvassing is important to the congregation, what takes place during a canvass call, program budget information, and guidelines to assist in making pledge decisions. It is important that both motivational and informational communication take place. Congregations often make the mistake of assuming that informational communication motivates. It does not.

Motivational communication needs to constantly remind members why they need to support the congregation's programs and ministry. The why is a shared vision or mission and goals. A good communication plan that motivates should relate how the congregation's programs and ministry serve the community in reaching that vision or mission. Some congregations create a formal case statement that expresses the motivational message of their annual canvass. This statement is used in various communications, including the brochure. Whether or not you prepare a formal statement, communications regarding the annual canvass need to include a motivational message in a variety of formats and forums.

Information about the annual canvass process itself needs to be provided to the congregation at least every other year. New members, especially those previously unaffiliated with a religious body or who come from other than

Protestant denominations, may not know that the congregation is financed by member contributions, that pledges are a promise to make a contribution, or that the canvass is the way to obtain pledges. We often assume that members understand how much money is needed from them when they may have no knowledge of this aspect of congregational life. The informational portion of canvass communication is important to educate new members and inform all members about annual fundraising.

In your canvass communication, stress the important role that pledging plays in congregational planning. All congregations need to know how much income they will receive each year so they can plan activities and make financial commitments to employees and programming costs. Knowing the level of pledging and future income helps congregational leaders make effective decisions. Encourage members who are reluctant to make a pledge commitment to do so rather than contribute to the plate collection.

Information Styles

People use three primary information processing modes: visual (images, printed words); auditory (sounds, spoken words); and kinesthetic (feeling, action). In any group of people, individuals will differ in their preferred modes of learning. Thus, important information needs to be communicated in different ways to reach these three different learning styles. For example, if important information is communicated by letter, people who prefer auditory or kinesthetic styles are not as likely to absorb the information as people who prefer a visual style.

When developing communications for an annual canvass, consider all the communication paths within the congregation. Most congregations include the following:

- Newsletter
- Sunday Order of Service
- Posters
- Letters
- Announcements from the pulpit

- Bulletin boards
- Sermon
- Flyers
- Announcements at social hour
- Announcements in committee meetings
- Skits
- Signs (at places that will benefit from the annual canvass)
- Gossip.

Communications about the annual canvass need to use as many paths as possible within the congregation. This will respond to members' different learning styles and provide multiple information exposure to ensure information awareness. It will also challenge creative people to use these paths in ways that will gain special attention and interest in the annual canvass.

Canvass Brochure

Many congregations find it helpful to prepare and publish a canvass brochure. The contents of a canvass brochure should include important motivational and informational communication for the annual canvass. It needs to articulate the congregation's vision or mission and the relationship of the canvass to that vision. It also needs to provide guideline information to assist members in making their pledge decision. (See Appendix 6 for more information about brochures.)

The challenge and value of a brochure is to develop this information in a concise, attractive, and easy-to-read document. A brochure can be prepared at a reasonable cost with electronic publishing capabilities. It need not be elaborate; a simple design may make it more effective. A brochure can be the single most important piece of literature in an annual canvass. It can be used multiple times as a mailing piece or insert, as well as a handout or literature rack document.

A brochure should be available for distribution at least one month and preferably two months before the start of an annual canvass. This length of time is needed to provide opportunities for multiple exposures of the brochure to congregation members.

Information Exposure

Everyone is bombarded today with information from many sources—television, radio, newspapers, billboards, mail posters, loudspeaker announcements, and many others. Being exposed to such a large quantity of information, people learn to tune out or ignore much of it. A rule of thumb used in some advertising circles is that on the average a person has to be exposed to information six to ten times to ensure that he or she has received it.

Although information from the congregation is important to its members, that information competes with all the other data members are receiving in their homes. To be understood, important information from the congregation needs to be communicated multiple times. As I mentioned earlier, using a theme and logo as part of each written communication provides a visual identification of annual canvass materials. It acts much like a trademark for commercial products and it makes the written piece stand out from all the other writings competing for attention.

7. The Canvass Goal and Giving Guidelines

An annual canvass bears a close relationship to a congregation's annual budget process. For most congregations, the fulfillment of pledges from an annual canvass is the greatest source of income. Thus the results of an annual canvass have a strong effect on a congregation's budget; likewise the budget process may have a strong effect on an annual canvass.

Chapter 12 of *The Congregational Handbook* describes in detail the mission budget process recommended for Unitarian Universalist congregations. Many congregations develop a preliminary mission budget by involving their religious communities to determine what is needed in annual canvass pledges. When the annual canvass is completed, the final budget is developed and program commitments are made based on the pledges received. Embedded in this process is the articulation of motivations for giving. Congregations that involve their members in dialogues to create a mission budget have already created motivation for generous pledging in an annual canvass.

The fundraising goals of an annual canvass are usually determined by congregational leadership and the Annual Canvass Committee the month or two before the canvass is launched. Fundraising goals usually include the total amount of pledges and the number of pledges in the annual canvass. For most members of a congregation, reaching a numbered goal in itself is not motivation to make a generous pledge. Showing pledging results measured against the goals simply informs the congregation of progress. But a goal does provide some motivation to the canvass team and congregational leadership because they have an emotional investment in the success of the annual canvass.

When deciding on your goal, here are some factors to consider:

- Projected needs from preliminary budget deliberations.

- Commitment to the shared vision or mission as expressed by congregational input into budget deliberations.
- The past few years' pledging results coupled with information about how those canvasses were carried out.
- Evaluation of the total giving capacity of the congregation (see Appendix 1: Financial Evaluation of the Congregation).
- Quartile analysis of giving (see Appendix 2: Quartile Analysis and Projection).
- The risk tolerance of the congregation. Does it like the challenge of a stretch goal or does it want the assurance that comes with meeting a smaller goal?

Guidelines for Giving

As I mentioned in Chapter 6, one of the elements of a communication plan is to provide guidelines for giving. This information helps prospective contributors decide how much they want to give for the annual canvass. These guidelines are not motivational even though congregations sometimes highlight them as reasons for giving. Giving is from the heart, not the head. Guidelines also help a congregation to define their expectations, which are especially important for the following groups:

- New members from other faiths who might be familiar with very different fundraising styles and expectations. Many Jewish temples state the amount of money necessary for full membership. Some churches obtain most of their money from the collection plate. Others encourage tithing.
- New members who never have been a member of a congregation and have no idea of what is expected.
- New members who haven't been a member since childhood and might hold on to the image that a quarter in an envelope or the plate is sufficient.
- Long-term members who can but have never contributed much and need to be reminded to share the load in assuming membership. They also need to know how increases in costs to support expanding programming reflects in their share of those costs.

No guideline is effective unless it is placed in the context of a congregation's vision and program costs. Here are some suggested guidelines for giving:

- **Suggested Share Guide** (see Appendix 3: Suggested Share Giving Guide). This is a commonly used guide based on giving a certain percent of income. It has some value in providing a gross level giving; however, because each person's circumstances with respect to income and expenses are so different, many people cannot relate to this method.
- **Gift Table** (see Appendix 4: Gift Table). This table of giving ranges shows how many contributions within each range are required for members to reach a congregation's dollar objective. Everyone can relate to the gift table because it shows that there is room for contributions of all sizes. Members who have the capability to give large amounts see the need for their contributions. Members who cannot give much also feel empowered because they see a place on the table for their contributions.
- **Personal Testimony.** One of the most powerful methods of inspiring generosity is a member's personal testimony of his or her commitment to the congregation and why he or she is making a pledge. It is even more powerful if given in person in Sunday worship or any other congregational gathering. A personal testimony does more than communicate information; it provides a high emotional content to which many people in the congregation can relate.
- **Weekly Contributions.** By comparing weekly contributions to a common recreation or event, such as a night at the movies or a family pizza dinner, an annual pledge is placed in a more tangible perspective. It allows members to compare the values represented by the pledge to other activities.
- **Specific Increase Requests.** Some congregations like to ask past contributors to consider increasing their donations from a previous annual canvass. This can be done by simply asking for a percentage (10 percent, for instance) and relate it to the vision or mission it serves. Other ways of expressing requests for increases might include specific amounts for contributors of certain categories ($100 increase if last year's pledge was below $1,000, and 10 percent increase if last year's pledge was above $1,000). When requesting specific increases, it is important to remember that whatever is asked should be very clear to members.

Using an average pledge or average cost in any giving guideline is not recommended because it drives down generosity. A congregation needs a range of pledges to move toward its vision, from large pledges by committed members with financial resources to small pledges from those who do not have the resources or have less commitment. There is room for all pledges. Talking about averages discourages people who can give much larger amounts and people of limited means who wish to give larger amounts but cannot.

Some congregations suggest a specific pledge amount to each of their members during the canvass process. Suggested pledge amounts should be developed by a subgroup of the Annual Canvass Committee. The group should review all the previous year's pledges and estimate how much each member could pledge for the next year based on limited knowledge about each member's financial circumstances.

Two ways of communicating a suggested pledge amount are by mailing a letter to members just before the canvass and by recording this amount on a canvasser's list of members so that he or she can mention it during a canvass visit. Often canvassers are uncomfortable about discussing specific amounts of money, so this method of communication may be unreliable. Whatever method is used, a specific pledge amount is only a suggestion. You need to be careful with your wording so that it does not seem like a demand.

This method may seem pushy to some members, especially since the Annual Canvass Committee has no way of knowing every member's real financial situation. On the other hand, some members might welcome a suggested pledge amount, even if the final pledge decision does not reach what has been suggested. This can be especially true of new members who might not know how much to contribute. Using specific pledge amounts may be more successful in the advance gift canvass where larger contributors and canvassers are more used to that mode from working with schools and other nonprofit organizations.

Some congregations occasionally use challenge gifts to increase the level of giving. The concept is simple: A member or group of members offers to challenge the congregation by matching specific types of gifts and the Annual Canvass Committee incorporates the challenge in the canvass. An example would be to match any new gifts or increases over a previous year's gift on a one-for-one basis. The terms of a match are determined by the specific goals of the challenge. If you decide to use a challenge gift, it is important to make the terms of the match easy to understand for it to be effective. Congregation members also must feel that the challenge is sincere and not just a gimmick to raise contributions.

Whatever guidelines you set, remember to let people know that contributions can be made in a number of different ways and frequency, from cash or by personal check to stocks or other financial instruments. Envelopes should be provided for members who want to make weekly or monthly contributions, especially if they might be in cash form. Weekly or monthly payments can be encouraged because they seem less burdensome. If you want to receive contributions in the form of stock or other financial instruments, your congregation's treasurer needs to make arrangements with a brokerage firm to convert these instruments into cash.

Tax Benefits

For members who use Schedule A on their annual federal income tax, contributions to the congregation may be deducted as a charitable contribution. Contributions of appreciated securities may be of significant financial advantage. By giving appreciated securities to the congregation, a member may take a deduction for the appreciated amount of the securities and not pay the capital gains tax on the appreciation. To determine specific tax benefits, potential contributors should contact their own financial or tax advisor or attorney.

8. Recruiting Canvassers

Recruiting canvassers and canvassing team leaders is a very important activity of the Annual Canvass Committee. The following steps will assist you in pulling together a good canvasser team.

Develop a Written Description

When recruiting canvassers and canvassing team leaders, a written description of responsibilities and duties shows prospects exactly what will be expected. This information allows canvassers to make informed decisions, knowing that there will be no surprises or unexpected demands. Prospects are more likely to accept something that is well articulated rather than something vague. Here is an example of a canvasser description.

- A canvasser will personally visit three to five members or friends to talk about the congregation and solicit an annual pledge.
- A canvasser must be enthusiastic about and committed to the congregation and be willing and able to share these feelings in a face-to-face conversation with members and friends.
- A canvasser must possess good listening skills and be interested in getting to know others in the congregation.
- A canvasser should be willing to serve as an ambassador for the congregation, to provide information about its programs, activities, and goals, as well as to obtain information from others about their own needs and interests.
- A canvasser should be willing to make a generous pledge to the congregation, based on personal commitment and capability and to talk to peers

about doing the same. In doing so, the canvasser needs to be sensitive to the particular situations of others.

- A canvasser must attend one canvasser workshop. He or she will make three to five personal visits to members and friends, of no more than one hour each in length, within a two-week period. The total amount of time involved will be five to seven hours.
- A canvasser will receive a brochure and other information about the congregation's goals, programs, and financial objectives. In addition, he or she will be given the names, addresses, and phone numbers of people he or she will be visiting. Support will be offered in the form of a workshop to help build knowledge and skills in the canvass process and from the Annual Canvass Committee. A canvasser will report to a team leader.

Minimize the Number of Canvasser Visits

It is easier to recruit canvassers when they have to make fewer canvass visits. With three visits per canvasser, one-quarter of potential pledges need to be canvassers. This ratio increases the commitment to an annual canvass by having a large part of the congregation on the canvass team. Five visits seem to be the maximum number to expect of a canvasser.

Organize Teams

Create canvasser teams, each with a team leader. This organization assists the follow-up process. Rather than having the Canvass Chair follow-up with each canvasser, he or she can contact team leaders, who contact the canvassers. The teams should consist of no more than four to six canvassers each. Team leaders will canvass their canvassers, as the Canvass Chair will canvass the team leaders.

Identify Prospective Canvassers

Some to consider are:

- People in the congregation who are already committed and involved

- People who came to small group meetings and expressed an interest in the process
- New members who canvassed in their last congregation
- Parents of children in the religious education program
- Former board members and committee members
- Retired people who have the desire and time to commit
- Members who want to get to know others in the congregation.

Assigning Prospects

Take care in matching recruiters to prospects, making selections that provide the greatest likelihood of success.

Take the Time to Recruit, Not Just Ask

Recruiting canvassers, like the rest of the annual canvass, is based on motivating the recruits, not pressuring them. When you recruit canvassers face-to-face, you honor their value by showing how important you consider them. When recruiting, emphasize how the annual canvass assists the congregation in meeting its vision and goals and provide prospects with a canvasser description. Describe the duties—the opportunity to attend a canvasser workshop and the personal visits to three to five prospects—and explain the time commitment involved. Emphasize the support that will be available from the Annual Canvass Committee. Above all, do this enthusiastically, demonstrating that it is fun for Unitarian Universalists to get together and talk about their faith.

Keep Canvassers Informed

Once canvassers are recruited, they are part of a team. They are the pool from which future members of the Annual Canvass Committee can be drawn and may be candidates for congregational leadership positions.

Acknowledge Canvass Participation

During and after the canvass, do one or more of the following to acknowledge the work of those involved:

- Hold a social function for canvassers.
- List canvassers in your congregation's newsletter or other written communication, thanking them for their efforts.
- Publicly recognize canvassers during a worship service.
- Hold a celebration party at the completion of a canvass and recognize the canvassers.
- Ask for suggestions on how to do the job better next time and include these suggestions in planning the next campaign.
- Have the congregation covenant with canvassers during Sunday worship.

Canvassers, by participating in a canvasser workshop and by making a few canvass visits, become more committed to the congregation and develop into some of the most enthusiastic contributors to the annual canvass.

9. Organizing a Canvass

At the heart of an annual canvass process is the canvass call. A face-to-face canvass visit provides optimal results over the years. However, some congregations want a greater variety in their fundraising approaches so they alternate a face-to-face canvass with one of the other approaches described in Chapter 5 of this book.

A well-organized canvass helps develop good habits of giving within a congregation. Using an alternate method of asking for pledges one year or two after a successful face-to-face canvass often provides very good results. However, this may lead congregations to conclude that canvassing isn't necessary. Experience shows that more than two years without a traditional canvass may result in a decline in good giving habits. Likewise, congregations that have had a series of poor or mediocre annual fundraising drives often require more than one year of well-organized annual canvasses to develop good habits of giving in the congregation.

If an alternate method to canvassing is used, such as a mail request or personal request at a congregational function, be extremely careful when using a canvass call as a backup. Sometimes this transmits the message that if someone doesn't give now, he or she can expect a face-to-face canvass call, which indicates that the canvass call is more of a penalty than the fun, inspirational process it can be. Ensure that all the messages given about the canvass call are positive ones.

Matching Canvassers to Prospective Contributors

The Annual Canvass Committee needs to decide how to assign prospective contributors to canvassers. Some congregations assign contributors to canvassers who know them; others assign contributors to canvassers who do not know them. Some congregations allow canvassers to choose whom they will call by giving them a sheet of names from which they can mark their choices. The Annual Canvass Committee uses this sheet to make assignments.

There is some advantage in having larger contributors visited by canvassers who share that category of giving. Canvassers who can only make small pledges sometimes have difficulty talking with larger contributors. The advantage of an advance gift campaign is that larger contributors are canvassed by a select set of canvassers composed of larger givers and congregational leadership.

In most congregations a few contributors require special care when selecting a canvasser. Also, after assignments are handed out to canvassers, there must be room to revise matches a canvasser does not want for whatever reason.

Mail Canvassing

Every congregation has members and friends who have moved away but keep up their membership. A special letter needs to be written for this group of members to solicit their pledges by mail. Accompanying the letter should be a brochure, pledge card, and stamped return envelope. What works well is to recruit one or more canvassers to write personal notes on these letters. This creates some of the intimacy of a face-to-face canvass and certainly creates goodwill among that group of members.

The Canvasser Packet

Each canvasser should be furnished with a materials packet to assist in the canvass process. Many congregations use two-pocket folders filled with the following items:

- Pledge cards for each prospective contributor
- An information sheet with names, addresses, telephone numbers, and last year's pledge for each of the contributors
- A sheet to record questions, notes, or other significant information for the Annual Canvass Committee or the congregational leadership
- Copies of the canvass brochure

- Notepaper and envelopes to write thank-you notes
- A copy of the budget and other relevant financial material produced during the year for the canvasser's information and to answer questions
- Specific instructions on how to fill out the pledge card, whom to return the completed cards, whom to ask for questions or help, and other relevant information a canvasser might need
- Any handouts from the canvasser workshop that might give more information or some assurance
- Information on gifts of stock.

The packet should be available at the canvasser workshop to reinforce the information covered. If prospective contributor names are selected at the workshop, the final list of names should be available shortly afterward. It is important to be prompt in getting information to canvassers because it sets the expectation of promptness in the canvass itself.

The Canvasser Workshop

The canvasser workshop is an important aspect of the annual canvass process. Many congregations mistakenly call it "canvasser training." Although the canvasser workshop includes training for people who have never canvassed before, it also provides specific information on the current year's canvass, material to motivate canvassers, and information on how to make the process most fulfilling.

The goal of a canvasser workshop is to provide canvassers with sufficient information and motivation so that he or she is enthusiastic about making calls on fellow members of the congregation. The emphasis is on enthusiasm and commitment, not techniques and procedures.

Attending a canvasser workshop should be mandatory for canvassers. When recruiting a canvasser, the workshop must be emphasized as an opportunity to enrich the canvasser in his or her assignment, not as a requirement. Even with the workshop, the total time commitment the canvasser makes is only a few hours a year.

Part 3 goes into more detail about the canvasser workshop and provides presentation ideas and handouts. Varying workshop agendas and leaders from year to year adds interest, especially for canvassers who serve every year. Investigate resources in your congregation's district to create a workshop that will be a change of pace. New ideas and viewpoints are worth a small fee that an outside workshop facilitator might require.

Canvassing the Canvassers

Before canvassing, it is important for canvassers to make their own pledges. Canvassers will be more comfortable making a canvass visit and asking for a pledge if they have already made their own pledge.

In the days after the canvasser workshop(s), the Advance Gifts Chair should canvass advance gift canvassers. The General Canvass Chair should canvass team leaders who in turn will canvass the canvassers.

Pledges from Annual Canvass Committee members, team leaders, and canvassers can be included in the advance gift or leadership gift totals and announced to the congregation at a canvass kickoff event at the beginning of the general canvass.

10. The Kickoff Event

Many options exist for launching your fundraising efforts. The most common form of kickoff event is a fellowship dinner with entertainment. Breaking bread seems to draw people closer in community than almost any other activity.

The most important elements for a kickoff event are to be inclusive of as many members as possible and to be fun. To accomplish this, a kickoff event should be of no or modest cost so everyone can attend. Holding an event that is a financial-burden on any group of members prevents them from having a good time. To be most inclusive, encourage entire families. This means a menu that appeals to all ages. Special attention could be given to children by providing child care and a special children's program or activities. Some dinner options include the following:

- *Catered dinner*. A catered dinner, especially if the caterer takes care of the dishes, does not put too much burden on anyone. The cost could be absorbed by the congregation's budget (if planned for), subsidized by the budget, or paid for by attendees. The dinner does not have to be expensive; some caterers specialize in serving reasonably priced meals. An option is to ask members to contribute dessert specialties and to auction dessert recipes to help defray dinner costs.
- *Pot luck or contributory dinner.* This dinner is low cost; each member contributes a dish. Some groups assign food types (main course, vegetable, beverage, etc.), others truly take "pot luck." Some congregations have a thematic pot luck such as an "international" dinner.
- *Exchange dinner.* Two nearby congregations exchange dinners. One prepares and serves dinner for the other, then the reverse happens at a later date.

- *Restaurant or function hall.* A nearby restaurant or function hall may have the space and capability to serve a dinner at a reasonable cost.

Your kickoff event can be structured around the theme and logo of your annual canvass or some aspect of your congregation's vision or mission. Any program that is part of the event can relate strongly to or just acknowledge the annual canvass. Examples of entertainment at the event are talent shows, sing-alongs, parodies, humorous speakers, musical performances, or dancing.

The kickoff event is an opportunity to celebrate the results of an advance gift canvass if it has been held. This inspires remaining members to consider their pledges. Any special announcements about the canvass can be made at a kickoff event. It is wise to keep announcements short and sweet; the goal of the evening is fun and community. Some congregations have woven canvass themes and activities into humorous songs or skits, providing members with memorable entertainment.

Advance Gift Canvass Event

Many congregations that hold advance gift canvasses also organize an advance gift kickoff event. This is usually a low-key social affair honoring members who are leading contributors in the congregation. It can be coffee and dessert or a wine and cheese event in a member's home or small reception hall. Some congregations hold a small buffet meal. Remarks made at the event should be short and express the congregation's appreciation for members' generous support.

11. How to Make a Canvass Visit

The canvasser packet should have a pledge card or information sheet with basic information about prospective contributors: name, address, telephone number, and last year's pledge. In some congregations, additional information is provided such as a member's status, the number of years he or she has been in the congregation, the number of children in religious education, and their connections to the congregation such as committee memberships or program participation.

If you as a canvasser do not know the prospective contributor to whom you've been assigned and the canvasser packet has insufficient information, your first step is to find out something about that person by asking the canvasser team leader or a member of the Annual Canvass Committee. Having information about prospective contributors often makes it easier to call for a canvass visit appointment and to start a conversation during the visit.

Calling for an Appointment

After getting information on prospective contributors, call for an appointment. Because everyone has busy schedules, including yourself, it is best to call for an appointment as soon as you receive your assignments. If your congregation is running a well-organized canvass, and has developed a good communications plan, prospective contributors should already know about the canvass visit and why you would like to visit them.

When you make your initial call, be positive and enthusiastic over the telephone. Be flexible in scheduling a time and location for the visit. Consider meeting in a local coffee shop before work or on a Saturday. Do not attempt to conduct a canvass visit during Sunday morning coffee hour; a quiet place to sit down is important for dialogue to take place. Plan for your visit to last thirty to forty-five minutes. If prospective contributors are in a partnership, include both members in your visit so that a pledge decision can be made.

Some members may indicate that they do not want a canvass visit but would rather send in a pledge. Sometimes prospective contributors do not want to entertain the canvasser in their own home or they have a very busy schedule. If you are flexible in your meeting time and place, you may get a face-to-face visit. If you exhaust all possibilities and can't arrange a face-to-face visit, gladly accept a pledge over the telephone or send a pledge card so the contributor can return it to the church via mail or personal delivery. In this case, it is helpful to spend a few minutes on the phone in a conversation about the congregation and canvass.

The Canvass Visit

Most of your canvass visit should be devoted to talking about the congregation and what it means to both the prospective contributor and yourself. The purpose of this dialogue is to express feelings about the congregation, possibly evoking a greater sense of commitment in the contributor. Your visit may develop as follows:

1. *Introductions.* If you do not know the potential contributor(s), this is an opportunity to learn about each other.
2. *Sharing the vision.* After introductions, the best way to lead off the conversation is by asking an open-ended question about the congregation. Sometimes introductions will lead into a conversation so that a question is not needed. Here are some examples of opening questions:
   - "What program in the congregation is most important to you at this time?"
   - "What one thing would you like to see happen in this congregation next year?"
   - "What do you think was the major achievement of the congregation this past year?"

   The dialogue that follows is the most important part of your canvass visit. If you are scheduled for a thirty-minute visit, your conversation should last at least twenty-five minutes. Let the conversation take its own course as long as it stays on a subject related to the congregation. Your dialogue may move in the following directions: sharing of feelings, sharing of priorities, sharing of information, or listening to concerns or complaints.

If a prospective contributor expresses concerns or complaints, try to understand that your visit might be the only forum in which he or she feels safe to express them. Don't take these concerns or complaints personally. Try to listen, not defend. Ask your prospective contributor if he or she wants a concern or complaint passed on to the appropriate people in the congregation. Often a prospective contributor just needs to talk about it and doesn't want it to go any further. If he or she does want a concern or complaint passed on, record it on a note sheet in your canvasser packet and let your prospective contributor know that you will pass it to the appropriate people.

3. *Answering questions.* Many people, especially newer members, have questions about some aspect of congregational life. The answers to these questions can be springboards for sharing information and feelings. If you cannot answer a particular question, promise to get an answer and record the question on a note sheet in your canvasser packet. Be sure to follow up to see that an answer is returned.

4. *Asking for the pledge.* When your visit time is almost up, introduce the subject of the annual canvass with "As you know, this is the annual canvass," or a similar statement. Say a few words about this year's canvass (from information given out at the canvasser workshop) and then ask for a pledge. Your request can be a simple statement such as, "We would appreciate your considering a generous pledge for this coming year." Hand a pledge card to the contributor and ask him or her to complete the pledge. He or she might have questions, but if your congregation developed good communications in the months before the canvass, few questions should arise at this point.

5. *Thanking the contributor.* Once your prospective contributor has completed the pledge card, thank him or her for the generous pledge. This is the end of the canvass visit. Another thank you should be expressed as your parting statement.

What if a prospective contributor won't make a pledge amount decision now and wants to keep the card to send in later? The best strategy is for you to keep the card and offer to return at a later time to have the card signed. If you leave the card and it is not mailed in, you will have to remind the contributor about the card, which can be a potentially uncomfortable process for both you and the contributor.

6. *Pledge acknowledgment.* After your visit, write a personal note of thanks for the pleasant visit and the pledge. Use the note paper supplied in your canvasser packet. Turn in pledge cards as soon after your canvass visit as possible. Once the Annual Canvass Treasurer has received your pledge cards, your congregation office should formally acknowledge receiving the pledge and thank the contributor. This can be done in the form of an attractive note of acknowledgment and thanks, signed by an officer of the congregation. A prompt acknowledgment gives the contributor a message that his or her pledge is important. This response can reinforce the good feeling that was a result of the canvass visit.

12. Canvass Follow-up

Often when an annual canvass is completed, the Annual Canvass Committee breathes a sigh of relief and disbands. A new committee forms several months later for next year's campaign. With this approach to fundraising, some significant tasks go undone. Developing a culture in which the Annual Canvass Committee is a year-round activity provides the coverage for annual canvass follow-up tasks.

Evaluation

Running the annual canvass is a learning process. The best way to capitalize on this knowledge is to hold an evaluation session after the canvass is completed. The Annual Canvass Committee and canvassers should attend this session to provide as much input as possible. Ask two questions: "What went well this year and why?" and "What could we have done better this year and how?"

The first question will reinforce the positives. The Annual Canvass Committee should bask in its accomplishments and feel good about them. The "why" part of the question is meant to gain a better understanding of cause and effect in the fundraising process. The second question is asked in the positive. To look at only what went wrong can get into blame and result in hurt feelings.

For each of these questions, it is best to have a round-robin response (allowing each person in turn to make one comment during each round; comments continue until none remain), noting the responses on an easel pad to be transcribed later for distribution. It is important that no responses get lost; all are valuable. People who are unable to attend can submit their answers to these questions in writing.

The Annual Canvass Committee should keep these comments in front of them when planning the next year's annual canvass. Year after year, this evaluation can be one of the most important tools in sustaining effective annual fundraising efforts.

Canvass Completion

Even with the best organization and people, usually a few members have not been canvassed by the end of the canvass period. These people may be extremely busy, away, or unavailable for some reason. They may even be ill or have had a change of circumstance, which may require attention on the part of the congregation's leadership. Remember, canvassing is more than asking for pledges. A follow-up effort needs to be made to reach these members and provide closure for the annual canvass. The Follow-up Committee needs to take the lead in providing this closure for the canvass.

Pledge Follow-up

A good way to keep accurate records is to develop a method for tracking the fulfillment of pledges. Contributions made toward pledges need to be posted promptly. Each congregation member should receive at least quarterly accountings of their pledge fulfillment so that they don't lose track of their payments; the statement will help them keep their records current.

The Follow-up Committee needs to monitor pledge fulfillment and contact any member who appears to be falling behind in their payments. The call is *not* to collect payments, but to inquire if there are any extenuating circumstances related to their pledge. If a canvass pledge has been receiving regular statements, his or her reason for not paying is usually not forgetfulness. He or she might have experienced a change in financial circumstances. The follow-up call should remind a canvass pledger that his or her pledge is not a contractual commitment and that other arrangements can be made—a new pledge at a lower amount, deferred payment until later in the year, or canceling the pledge until financial circumstances improve. Sometimes a member who isn't paying his or her pledge is unhappy with some aspect of the congregation. Understanding this concern can allow appropriate resources to be applied to resolve the situation.

This intervention, done in a caring way, can often prevent a member from dropping out. Often when people cannot fulfill a pledge, they feel badly and are reluctant to initiate contact with the congregation. If this situation goes without intervention, these bad feelings can result in the member withdrawing from congregational activities and the congregation itself. Intervening in this way is another form of ministry.

New Member Orientation and Canvassing

As people join your congregation throughout the year, they need to be informed about the financial aspects of membership. The Annual Canvass Follow-up Committee should take part in whatever new member preparation the congregation holds (new member orientation, preparation classes, etc.). Some congregations hand out prepared brochures or other printed material on the financial aspects of membership. As with other canvass communications, the emphasis should be on the congregation's vision: where it is going and how contributions help get it there.

Another task of the Follow-up Committee is to canvass each of the new members before or after their induction. This initial canvass visit is much like the annual canvass visit, discussing what's important about the congregation. However, when talking with a new member it helps to spend more time providing information and answering questions.

Other Forms of Giving

The Follow-up Committee is also in a good position to encourage congregation members to consider gifts to endow the congregation. Gifts can be in the form of direct gifts, a charitable trust, or a bequest in a will. The Unitarian Universalist Association Development Department has a number of brochures and other material to assist you in presenting these options. The Unitarian Universalist Association also has in place charitable trusts your congregation can share rather than going to the expense and trouble to set up your own.

PART THREE

Learning to Be a Canvasser

13. The Canvasser Workshop

The canvasser workshop is an important learning experience. It provides tools for new canvassers to enjoy the canvass process and equips experienced canvassers with new ideas and enthusiasm for their canvass visits. This educational activity empowers canvassers by teaching the skills for an effective canvass call, instilling enthusiasm for the canvass process, relieving concerns or reservations, and providing important information about the canvass.

When recruiting canvassers, this workshop should be discussed as an integral part of their responsibilities and opportunities, not as an option. Even if you are recruiting an experienced canvasser, special information about this year's canvass and the vision underlying it, as well as new ideas to make the canvass fun, are introduced at these workshops. Any canvasser can benefit from its motivational aspects and from the feeling that he or she is part of an important team.

If your congregation has more than ten or twelve canvassers, it helps to schedule more than one workshop. This provides canvassers with a choice of times to attend and keeps the groups small enough to share information and ideas. Workshops can be scheduled in the evening or during a weekend. Two hours is the minimum time to allow for the workshop. To provide time for gathering and as many questions as possible, schedule two and one-half to three hours for the entire activity.

Canvasser workshops for both the advance gift canvass and the general canvass should be scheduled no more than two weeks before their beginning. This allows time after the workshops for canvasser pledging while keeping workshop information fresh.

Foster team feelings by creating a social mood. Refreshments can be served during the gathering and should also be available during a short break in the workshop. The layout of the room should be as informal as possible, with canvassers sitting in a single circle. The workshop facilitator should have an easel with a pad of paper, markers, and tape to display completed sheets on the wall. Writing is an important reinforcement of the spoken word. The combination of speaking, writing, and seeing the written word responds to the three learning styles mentioned in Chapter 6.

Have canvasser packets available at these workshops. Even if you do not have all the names of people to be canvassed, the packet is important because it has information that reinforces the material covered in the workshop. Also, handouts of key ideas discussed in the workshop can be helpful for canvassers to review later, closer to the canvass visit. Some handouts for a canvasser packet are included in this part.

The major topics of a canvasser workshop might include the following:

- Why canvassing is important—the sharing of commitment
- The goals of this annual canvass in terms of vision and mission
- The process of a canvass call from name assignment to thank-you note
- The procedures for reporting back to the Annual Canvass Committee
- Going through canvasser packets and explaining potential contributor assignments.

A sample workshop agenda could be:

- Introductions
- Concerns, fears, and questions
- Face-to-face canvass: capability and commitment, ministry and community, asking for the pledge
- Giving money—a positive experience
- The canvass process—six steps to successful canvassing
- Campaign procedures
- Wrap-up.

This suggested outline can be modified as your workshop dictates. It is helpful to distribute an outline to aid canvassers in remembering the discussion topics. The following sections are modules that can be used by facilitators of canvasser workshops.

Introductions

Every workshop should begin with an introduction of each person. In congregations with new canvassers, introductions help get everyone on a common basis. Even if everyone knows everybody else, introductions should be structured to reveal something new that builds further community, such as:

- Name
- How long have you been canvassing?
- What is the most important program or activity for you in the congregation today?
- Where do you envision the congregation to be five years from now?

The last two are examples of open-ended questions to get individuals to discuss their commitment and vision for the congregation. Opening the workshop with a commitment and vision sets the tone for later discussions. Writing down the key ideas that are mentioned reinforces the importance of these idea by putting them into visual form.

Concerns, Fears, and Questions

Often people who have never canvassed before, or who have had difficult experiences with it, come to canvasser workshops with concerns, fears, or questions. One technique used by some facilitators is to ask for them up front. He or she records each item on a large easel pad and states that by the end of the workshop, each issue will be addressed. Near the end of the workshop, the sheet is displayed again and items taken care of are checked off. Items not checked off are then discussed.

The principle behind this process is that if people unload their concerns and questions at the beginning of the session, they are more likely to pay attention to the workshop, knowing that their items will be addressed during the session.

Face-to-face Canvass

Given a selection of worthy organizations asking us for money to meet valid needs, what motivates us to choose the recipients of our contributions? To answer this question, ask workshop participants to respond and record their comments on an easel pad. Have the group look at the common thread in their responses.

It will become evident that the responses are primarily emotional, that most people use an emotional basis in making their choices. The conclusion that can be drawn from this discussion is that the annual canvass process is rooted in appealing to the emotions, not simply asking for money. The Unitarian Universalist way of fundraising emphasizes positive motivations, appealing to feelings that enable prospects to choose the congregation as a recipient of their contributions.

Capability and Commitment

Draw a simple chart on an easel pad with one horizontal line along the bottom and one vertical line up the center of the sheet labeled "$" at the top. Label one side of the chart "Capability," the other "Commitment." Explain that these are the two major factors that influence how much members contribute to the congregation. A person with high capability and low commitment will not give a large amount of money; neither will someone with low capability and high commitment. The largest contributors are people with high capability and high commitment. They are the prospective contributors canvassed in an advance gift canvass. The purpose of a canvass is to get members to articulate their commitments and to evoke in them a greater sense of their commitment, which often leads to higher contributions.

Building Community

What takes place during a canvass visit? Lead a discussion on this question and capture responses on an easel pad. Mention characteristics such as listening, caring, sharing, teaching, and others. Show how the visit between a canvasser and a prospective contributor can be a bonding process in which respective feelings and commitment are shared. If a canvasser and contributor did not know each other before the call, they will develop a relationship, if not a friendship. If they know each other, they will strengthen that bond. A canvass in which every member is called on builds many lasting links in the faith community.

Ministry

What is ministry? You may want to lead a discussion similar to the one for building community, capturing the responses on an easel pad. The responses will be amazingly alike. In your discussion, point out that the canvass process is a ministry of the congregation and that canvassers are an integral part of this ministry.

Giving Money—A Positive Experience

Workshop participants may say that discomfort with talking about or asking for money is a major fear or concern. Here are some suggestions for discussing this subject:

- Share different concepts of money as provided in this manual or as expressed in Jacob Needleman's *Money and the Meaning of Life*.
- Ask workshop participants to think about where these concerns or fears might come from. (Very often it comes from childhood when parents have cautioned them about discussing family financial affairs with others. Articulating these roots of concerns or fears will help raise the comfort level in talking about money.)
- Ask participants if anyone has unwisely spent money and whether they purchased something of poor quality or something disappointing. Have them describe what it was and how they felt about it. Then ask participants to discuss something of good value that they have recently purchased. Ask them how they feel when they have spent their money wisely. The good feeling that comes with a wise expenditure is how people should feel when they contribute to their congregation—it is a good value. This is how contributors should feel after a canvass visit—that they have made a wise investment. The successful canvass is one in which both the canvasser and the contributor feel good after the canvass visit.

Canvass Procedures

In this phase of the canvasser workshop, the Annual Canvass Chair or other canvass committee member should provide procedural information about the canvass:

- canvass organization
- description of pledge cards
- canvassing the canvassers
- contents of canvasser packet
- turning in pledge cards
- answering questions
- other information.

This information should also be in written form as part of the canvasser packet for their reference. When preparing written and verbal instructions, materials should be clear and complete. Poorly composed or incomplete instructions will leave canvassers feeling unsupported and can undermine a successful canvass.

14. Canvasser Resources

Three resources in this chapter—An Interview With a Purpose, Six Steps to Successful Canvassing, and How to Deal With Common Questions—are handy tips to discuss at a canvasser workshop or to keep in a canvasser packet.

An Interview With a Purpose

The oldest, most universal method people have used to assess one another is interviewing. It is a good way to get to know another person. If it is done with skill and sensitivity, interviews allow people to discover and share commonly held beliefs and values and to arrive at a clearer understanding of one another. Effective interviewing ensures that the interchange will be a productive, enlightening, and rewarding experience.

In *The Effective Management of Volunteer Programs*, Marlene Wilson writes that the qualities that effective interviewers need are: an ability to converse easily with others, acceptance of all people, skills in observing or sensing other people accurately, knowledge of the task at hand and the institution you serve, the ability to speak clearly and explain things well, the capacity to recognize and acknowledge other people's concerns, the ability to guide the conversation effectively without sacrificing sensitivity or purpose.

This is a lot to think about and evaluate. We probably will not be endowed with every one of these attributes, but by being aware of them we can do a significantly better job of conducting our canvass visits. One of the best ways to get to know someone is to ask qualitative, not quantitative, questions. For example, saying "tell me about your family" will get you a much more informative response than merely asking, "How many children do you have?" Likewise, you will be better served by saying, "Tell me about your hopes and dreams for this church," than by asking, "How long have you been a member?"

Six Steps to Successful Canvassing

1. Make your own generous pledge. As a canvasser you cannot help others identify with their own commitment if you have not done so yourself. Your own experience in making this decision and your own enthusiasm for the congregation can be a part of the canvass conversation.

2. Call ahead for an appointment. Most people today are too busy to appreciate a canvasser who drops in unannounced. Call the person or family to arrange a mutually agreeable time. Make sure the person understands that you are coming to canvass. If this is a family pledge, try to arrange a time when both partners can be present.

If the donor resists your visit, try to arrange a face-to-face, private visit somewhere else: at your home or a nearby coffee shop. Avoid meeting at church; you'll be too rushed and it will be difficult to have a private conversation in most churches on Sunday.

If the person is still reluctant, emphasize that the canvass visit is an important time for members and friends to share information about their experiences in the church. Offer to make the visit brief if time is a concern (and make sure you do so). If the person has made a decision, tell them you would be glad to come by to accept their pledge.

3. Know your prospect. Before you visit, learn something about the person or family you will be visiting. Is this a new family or a long-term member? Do they have children? Do they serve on any committees? Have they participated in any congregational events? What are their interests? What has been their level of pledging? What should you be prepared to suggest to them about their pledge?

If this information is not available to you, open the canvass visit with these questions and listen to the responses. The person will tell you valuable things about the congregation and his or her involvement in it.

4. Engage in a face-to-face discussion of the person's interest and feelings about the congregation. Have some questions ready for conversation starters, such as "What program in our congregation is most important to you?" or "What one thing in our congregation has meant the most to you this year?" or "What one thing would you like to see happen in our congregation next year?" Feel free to share your own story and the process in which you made your own pledge. Offer to answer questions about the congregation, the plans for the upcoming year, the budget, etc. If you do not know the answers, offer to find them. If the person has concerns or ideas, make a note of them and offer to share them, with the person's permission, with the appropriate congregational officers or staff. This conversation is the most important part of your visit because it assists the donor in realizing her or his depth of commitment to the congregation and understanding what is a fair pledge. This process builds community and performs a ministry.

5. **Ask for the pledge.** Do this when the person or family is ready. If you are not sure they are ready to pledge, simply ask. Hand them their pledge card and ask them to consider a generous pledge. Offer to answer any questions about the pledge. If they need more time to discuss or think about their pledge, do not leave the pledge card. Offer to come back with the pledge card so they may complete and sign it.

Note: Leaving the pledge card behind creates logistical problems for a canvasser. Well-meaning members often put off making the pledge decision or forget to mail or bring in the pledge card. This puts you in the position of calling to remind them and of not being able to meet the deadlines set by the canvass organization. It is much better not to give the pledge card to donors until they are ready to pledge. Make a date for a second meeting, if necessary. This will create a deadline. When doing so, give two positive choices: "I'm free on Tuesday or Saturday morning, which is better for you?"

Be responsive to special circumstances and express your gratitude on behalf of the congregation when the decision has been made.

6. **Say thank you. Say thank you again!** Remember: You are building a community. You are building a ministry. Have fun!

Dealing With Specific Situations

Situation 1

Contributor (on phone, when you call to set up a visit): "You don't need to come, we know what we're giving this year. Just send me a card."

You: "Your pledge is very important to us and I really enjoy taking the time to come see you! It will give us an opportunity to talk about our congregation and what it means to us. Will ____ o'clock be convenient for me to stop by for your signature?"

Situation 2

Contributor: "I'd rather not have someone come to my home."

You: "Why don't we meet at the ______ Coffee Shop next Saturday morning? It's reasonably quiet and easy to get to."

Situation 3

Contributor: "Why do I have to pledge? Why can't I just make a contribution when I come to the service?"

You: "Our congregation needs pledged money commitments from its members and friends so that it can plan its expenditures and make the necessary commitments to fulfill the programming for next year. You can pay in weekly, monthly, or any other installments that you choose."

Situation 4

Contributor: "The canvass needs rather large pledges. I spend a lot of time working on our congregation's committees. Shouldn't I be able to pledge less when I give so much in other ways."

You: "We very much appreciate all the work you have done, and it's been very valuable. However, we do need your financial support as well as your time and talent. Many of the members who give the most time are also its biggest pledgers, giving substantial amounts of money."

Situation 5

Contributor: "I'd rather not pledge now because I'm expecting to be transferred."

You: "We would still like a pledge based on a full year to assist us in our planning. If you move, we would expect you to pay only the amount attributable to the part of that time spent here. A pledge is not a legal obligation."

Situation 6

Contributor: "I've decided to decrease my pledge because I don't like (the minister, plan, the board, the social activities, etc.)."

You: "We're sorry you feel that way. If you'd like, tell me more about your objections. I'll be sure to inform the appropriate people. This feedback is valuable." (*Do write the objection down and follow through by advising the campaign chair, who will see that the right person is informed and a response is sent.*)

Situation 7

Contributor: "How soon must I pay my pledge?"

You: "The pledge period runs for one year. You may choose any payment schedule that suits you. We appreciate knowing your intentions, for planning purposes."

Situation 8

Contributor: "May I pay my pledge in stock?"

You: "Of course. If it is appreciated stock, you can send the stock, endorsed over to the congregation, to our treasurer. We will take care of the rest. You may well get favorable tax treatment on the contribution. If the stock has depreciated since purchase, you would be better off selling it yourself so that you can take the tax loss and donate the proceeds to the congregation."

Situation 9

Contributor: "I'm not sure how well our family finances are going to hold up during the next year. What if I make a pledge and then find I can't honor it?"

You: "You can always revise your pledge. We hope you will be as generous as you can in supporting our congregation, but we recognize that circumstances do change."

Afterword

Money and the Minister

When I began my ministry, I brought all my anxieties about money with me. It's not my responsibility to raise money, I thought. That's someone else's job. I'm doing what I do as a minister, and the congregation ought to take care of my compensation. Why aren't they doing more . . . and better?

Although a strong advocate for "every member canvassing," I made clear early in my ministry that I had no role to play in the canvass process. Financing the congregation is the responsibility of the congregation, not the minister, I thought. In retrospect, oddly I did feel responsible enough to participate in budget committee deliberations, but I took no part in finance or canvass committee meetings.

When I look back on those first years, I see now that I carried a confused and conflicted understanding of money. As the minister, helping professional, counselor, worship leader, and spiritual guide, I transmitted both overtly and covertly my confusion and conflict to the congregation and its leadership.

In the seven years since my ministry began with the Unitarian Universalist Fellowship of Falmouth, Massachusetts, I have undertaken a more open and intentional aproach to money. I have learned to speak from the pulpit and at coffee hour, in committees and on the telephone, about the symbolic power of money, whose meanings we must work to discern and nurture.

Congregational health, both spiritual and material, is sustained and nurtured through a generous, liberal, and liberating vision of service to others. Members of our congregations take up and are taken up in such visions. Hope, trust, and enthusiasim are released from the stone-cold chill that numbs the spirit.

Because congregations need clarity from the confusion and conflict they experience over money, candid leadership from ministers is irreplaceable. One task of ministerial leadership is to help members and friends feel proud of their financial giving. To get that clarity, both ministers and congregations need to speak of their expectations and to ask for what they want. The most obvious time to seek the foundations of this clarity is during the settlement process. Once called and installed, the minister and the congregation will face constant challenges in discerning the values and meanings of money. Some of the most obvious and continuing of these challenges include the weekly offering and the annual operating canvass.

The weekly offering is a sacrament of the free church. This sacrament calls forth the regular and voluntary generosity of all who join our congregations, and it is an opportunity and invitation to members and friends to release themselves from the crush of wealth and power that burden and suffocate the spirit.

Liberal religious communities call for the Sunday offering as a regular and visible invitation to sustain and strengthen the church, fellowship, and society that is precious to so many: Our religious communities are places of memory and hope, and their members are keepers of the dream.

When given and received, the weekly offering expresses the spiritual dimensions of money in grateful appreciation of our shared hopes and values. It also challenges the oppression and repression of secularity.

The annual operating canvass is a way for the congregation to share its joys and concerns and to give to the service of its hopes and dreams. When this special sharing is gathered and returned to the congregation through its leadership, then the canvass becomes a prayer for the new year.

The operating canvass situates the congregation in the present while glancing backward and looking forward. By examining how we are doing in our ministry, the annual canvass invites every member to share hopes, explain problems, ask for gifts, and thank one another. Sharing, explaining or reasoning, asking, and thanking is truly a fundamental paradigm for all congregational life.

Visible ministerial support to a congregation's efforts to plan, implement, and evaluate an annual canvass is a fundamental expression of cooperation. (How much the minister may or may not participate in canvassing itself is always a negotiable point.) Moreover, appropriate and visible giving by the minister models healthy participation for the congregation, and it places credible foundation stones under the congregation's vision.

The invitation to share and to hope is essential, but when canvassers are impulsed by allurement or fear, then the congregation's prayer for a new and generous year goes unarticulated and gives way first to irreverence and then to irrelevance.

My seven years with the Unitarian Universalist Fellowship of Falmouth have been challenging, difficult, and even painful ones as my congregation and I endeavored to fashion a Unitarian Universalist presence in our community. Over and over again, confusion and anxiety about money knotted our efforts. However, we are also a gifted community who have had the good sense and good will to accept the gifts of the spirit that are ours.

In my years of ministry to and with my congregation, the average pledge to our operating budget has quadrupled, we undertook a successful capital campaign that exceeded our goals, and we have experienced ourselves as a gifted, successful, and generous congregation. My understanding about money evolved and my involvement with fundraising increased in the following ways:

- **Settlement.** As part of my settlement, the congregation and I promised to keep good faith with one another: I to remain in good standing with the Ministerial Fellowship Commitee, and the congregation to make its annual fair-share contributions to both the Associaion and district. These promises anchored our relationships within the covenant of the Unitarian Universalist Association.

- **Pledging.** My wife and I have consistently pledged above the congregation's average for both the operating and capital drives. But because my readiness to pledge has not always corresponded with my wife's willingness, we have negotiated and renegotiated our pledging. Our differences, not very different from those of other couples in the congregation, demanded attention in order to make our gifts.

- **Advocacy.** I have written about and spoken to the importance of a vision for our community—*from* the pulpit to our annual every-member canvass, *to* the Governing Board, and *at* various budget, canvass, and finance meetings. However, simple speech has not been enough in itself, and I believe that sharing my personal enthusiasm and hopeful expectation was as important as my words.

- **Presentation.** To discipline my own thinking and actions, I facilitated canvass training for other congregations and I presented workshops envisioning the abundance of our material and spiritual gifts.
- **Representation.** I carried the vision and financial opportunities of my congregation to the leadership of the district and its other congregations. In particular, I collaborated with key district leadership to advance understanding and to take responsibilities for our Association's covenant, "promising to one another our mutual trust and support."

When looking across these eventful years, several gifts of the spirit have served us well: a *vision* of whom we want to become as a people; the *courage* to take risks on behalf of our vision, which in time became *trust* among ourselves that we had not known before; and *forgiveness* when we did not live up to each other's expectations.

Congregations and their ministers deserve to understand the value and meaning of money. Meaning, however, is not created by magic, but by diligent and respectful exchanges between congregation and minister. The meaning and value of money are threaded, one way or another, in the vision of the congregation. This thread is properly used to knit hope and service, trust and mercy, not to strangle generosity.

When a vision of hope and trust exists, transformation is possible, and money, along with all the other material and spiritual gifts of our members, gladly follows in step with the spirit. And then we are free to do justice, show mercy, and create anew.

The Reverend David Nash Williams
Unitarian Universalist Fellowship
Falmouth, Massachusetts

Appendix

1. Financial Evaluation of the Congregation

Income Evaluation

The evaluation process is an important step in the Annual Fund Campaign. The purpose is to give the congregational leadership and the Annual Canvass Committee an idea of the true annual giving potential of the congregation. It is done by estimating the income range of each pledging unit to arrive at a total income for the congregation.

The evaluation is best performed by a small task group of three to five people from the congregation who collectively have a good knowledge of the congregation's members and friends. This group might include the minister, the annual canvass chair, the congregational board chair, and at least one important contributor.

Before the task group meeting, prepare a card for each pledging unit by writing the name(s), address, and past year's pledge on the card. Do the following steps.

1. Develop a set of income ranges to use in sorting the name cards. A suggested list of ranges follows, but can be modified depending on the profile of annual income ranges within the congregation:

$0	to	$15,000	$50,000	to	$70,000
15,000	to	25,000	70,000	to	100,000
25,000	to	35,000	100,000	to	150,000
35,000	to	50,000	150,000		and up

2. The task group estimates the gross annual income for each of the pledging units by turning up a card and jointly deciding the income range for that pledging unit and placing that card in the pile representing that range. The estimate is based on knowing the occupation(s) represented in the

pledging unit and the range of pay for those occupations. Other factors entering into the estimate might include known capital resources such as inheritance and ownership interests, and neighborhood of residence. It has to be emphasized that this is just an estimate for evaluation purposes; the group cannot have exact knowledge of a member's financial resources. No more than twenty to thirty seconds per card are necessary to decide.

If there is no knowledge of a particular pledging unit within the group, the card can be placed into an unclassified pile. At the end of the decision step, the group decides how to get enough information in a reasonable time to assign those cards.

3. Count the cards in each pile. Multiply the number of cards in each pile by the median income that pile represents to obtain a total gross income for each income range. Then add the total obtained for each pile to obtain a grand total. This represents an estimate of the total gross income of the congregation.
4. Divide last year's annual fund pledge or actual total by the total gross income to determine the percentage of total income your congregation actually contributed.
5. Multiply the gross income by a percentage target to obtain the estimated giving capacity for the congregation. Two or two and one-half percent is a reasonable percentage to use as the multiplier. Divide the estimated giving capacity by the number of pledging units used to obtain the required average contribution per pledging unit.

   The numbers obtained show a reasonable amount of potential for giving within the congregation and how far the congregation has to go to reach that potential. Most congregations are surprised at how much that is potentially available is not being realized.

Use of Analysis Sheets

Calculating This Year's Canvass Potential

1. Count each stack of cards and enter the number on the appropriate income range line in column 3, "# Pledge Units," on the Congregation Evaluation Worksheet on page 94.

2. Multiply the number of cards in column 3 by the median income in column 2 for each income range, then put the answers in column 4. This gives the total income within each income range.
3. Decide which percentage share of income you feel is fair for that income range.
4. Multiply the total income in column 4 by the percent share in column 5 for each income range, then put the answers in column 6. This gives the "giving potential" for each range.
5. Add the figures in column 6 and place the answer in the total line at the bottom of the column, giving the total giving potential.

Evaluation of Last Year's Canvass

1. Count the number of cards in each stack of those who pledged last year and enter in the appropriate income range line in column 7.
2. Multiply the number in column 7 by the median income in column 2 and put the answers in column 8. This gives the total income of those who pledged last year for each income range.
3. Add up the *actual* pledges from last year in each stack of cards and put on the appropriate line in column 9.
4. Divide the actual contributions in column 9 by the total income in column 8 and put the answers in column 10. This figure is the percent share actually received last year for each range. Compare this figure to the percent share in column 5.

Congregation Evaluation Worksheet

		This Year				Last Year			
Col. 1	Col. 2	Col. 3	Col. 4	Col. 5	Col. 6	Col. 7	Col. 8	Col. 9	Col. 10
Income Range	Median Income	# Pledge Units	Total Income	% Share	Giving Potential	# Pledge Units	Total Income	Actual Contribution	% Share
TOTALS									
		# of Pledges	Col. 2 x Col. 3	Applied Percent	Col. 4 x Col. 5	# of Pledges	Col. 2 x Col. 7	Total of Pledges	Col. 9/ Col. 8

2. Quartile Analysis and Projection

This is a valuable technique for analyzing the results of an annual canvass and projecting future canvass results. The basic premise is that different size pledges come from different segments of the congregation. If it has a hundred pledging units or more, the distribution of pledges is predictable, based on data from many successful canvasses in many congregations.

The Quartile Distributions are as follows:

- 25% of total is given by the 5% pledging the largest amount
- 25% of total is given by the 10% pledging the next largest amount
- 25% of total is given by the 20% pledging the next largest amount
- 25% of total is given by the 65% pledging the least amount

Thus it is expected that 15% of the congregation will pledge one half of the annual canvass total, while the other one half is usually pledged by the remaining 85% of the congregation.

The Quartile Method can be used to:

- Determine which constituencies in your congregation have the potential for increasing their pledges, thus allowing you to concentrate your efforts on them during the next canvass.
- Assist in setting a realistic goal for your next canvass based on identifiably strong areas.
- Provide data useful in setting up a gift table. (See Appendix 4.)
- Check on the evaluation process.

Using the Quartile Method to Evaluate Canvass Results

1. On the Quartile Analysis Worksheet on page 98, list your canvass goal next to "Total" at the bottom of column 2, "Goal Forecast."
2. Divide your canvass goal by four and place the result in each of the quartile rows in column 2. For example, on the Sample Worksheet: $84,000/4 = $21,000 in Quartile rows 1, 2, 3, and 4.
3. Place the forecasted number of pledging units under "Total" at the bottom of column 5, "Pledge Unit Forecast." On the Sample Worksheet it is 252.
4. Calculate 5% of the total pledge unit forecast (for example, .05 X 252 = 13), placing the result in the Quartile 1 row of column 5, "Pledge Unit Forecast." Do the same for Quartiles 2 through 4 using the percentages in column 4, "Percent Pledge Units."
5. Create a list of all the pledges from the canvass in order of the pledge amount, the highest on top and the lowest on the bottom.
6. Count the number of pledges on the list and place this number under "Total" in column 6, "Pledge Unit Actual." Then fill in the quartile rows in the same column, placing 5% of the total in Quartile 1, 10% in Quartile 2, 20% in Quartile 3, and the remainder 65% in Quartile 4.
7. Using the number you placed in Quartile 1 of column 6, count down that many pledges from the top of the list of pledges. Draw a line on the list separating this top group from the rest: continue counting down the list, doing the same with the numbers in column 6 for Quartiles 2, 3, and 4.
8. For each quartile group on the list, add the dollar amounts of the pledges to get a total for each group, then place that figure in the appropriate quartile row in column 3, "Goal Actual."
9. Now examine the chart. The second column, "Goal Forecast," and the third column, "Goal Actual," will give you a comparison of what each of the Quartile groups actually contributed compared to a normal, successful canvass. Not every congregation will have the same profile, of course, nor will any congregation exactly match the Quartile comparison. What to look for are significant variations between the actual

dollar amounts in each Quartile and those that were forecast, giving thoughtful consideration of the possible cause(s). This can be especially helpful in planning next year's canvass.

For example, if your congregation reaches its goal of X number of pledging units but falls short of its goal in terms of the total dollars raised, the quartile analysis can show you where the weaknesses are, that is, one or two of the groups may have fallen short of the forecast by a considerable amount. This would tell you that in all likelihood those groups have not been adequately reached: Perhaps the communications effort was incomplete, the message not articulated, or the canvassing process was not done as well as it could have been.

As another example, if your canvass reached its goal and one or more groups pledged higher than forecast, it may well be that the canvass goal was set too low.

Using the Quartile Method to Forecast a Canvass

1. Using a new worksheet, perform steps 5 through 8 on the list above using actual data from your last canvass.
2. Review the quartile groups that performed significantly below their 25% of the total and plan the steps you can take to bring them to expectations. Among these may be more effective communications, a greater sense of vision and/or mission, or even an improved canvass organization.
3. Fill in the Goal Forecast column based on the previous year's actual results and complete the Pledge Unit Forecast column to provide the profile for the new canvass.

Quartile Analysis Worksheet

Col. 1	Col. 2	Col. 3	Col. 4	Col. 5	Col. 6
Quartile	Goal Forecast	Goal Actual	Percent Pledge Unit	Pledge Unit Forecast	Pledge Unit Actual
1			5		
2			10		
3			20		
4			65		
Total			100		

Sample Quartile Analysis Worksheet

Col. 1	Col. 2	Col. 3	Col. 4	Col. 5	Col. 6
Quartile	Goal Forecast	Goal Actual	Percent Pledge Unit	Pledge Unit Forecast	Pledge Unit Actual
1	$21,000		5	13	
2	$21,000		10	25	
3	$21,000		20	50	
4	$21,000		65	164	
Total	$84,000		100	252	

3. Suggested Share Giving Guide

An example of a Suggested Share Giving Guide is given below. You can adjust the percentages for each category as the circumstances in your congregation indicate.

Gross Income	Helping %	Helping Annual Amount	Helping Weekly Amount	Supporting %	Supporting Annual Amount	Supporting Weekly Amount	Sustaining %	Sustaining Annual Amount	Sustaining Weekly Amount
$10,000	1.00	$104	$2.00	1.50	$156	$3.00	2.00	$208	$4.00
20,000	1.50	312	6.00	2.00	390	7.50	2.50	468	9.00
30,000	2.00	624	12.00	2.50	780	15.00	3.00	939	18.00
40,000	2.25	936	18.00	2.75	1,092	21.00	3.25	1,300	25.00
50,000	2.50	1,300	25.00	3.00	1,560	30.00	3.50	1,820	35.00
75,000	3.00	2,080	40.00	3.50	2,600	50.00	4.00	3,120	60.00
100,000	3.50	3,500	67.00	4.00	4,000	77.00	4.50	4,500	87.00

To determine income:

Start with Adjusted Gross Income (Line 31 of IRS Form 1040) __________

Add: Preference Income

- Tax-exempt pensions and annuities __________

- Tax-free income ___________
- Depreciation on rental property ___________
- Other ___________

Total Additions ___________

Deduct:

- Non-reimbursed major medical expenses ___________
- Care of parent(s) ___________
- Costs of higher education ___________
- Costs of child care ___________

Total Deductions ___________

INCOME for use in determining share ___________

4. Gift Tables

A useful communication tool for the annual fund campaign is the gift table, a grouping by dollar value of the expected gifts from the congregation. An example of a gift table is shown here.

Gift Table

Range	Number	Value
Over $5,000	3	$12,500
$2,000 - $5,000	6	$21,000
$1,000 - $2,000	19	$28,500
$700 - $1,000	28	$23,800
$500 -$700	40	$24,000
$300 - $500	36	$14,400
$100 - $300	24	$4,800
Under $100	10	$1,800
Totals	**166**	**$130,800**

The gift table allows the contributors to see where their pledge will fit among the variety and number of campaign pledges required. Some congregations mention the average contribution size needed for the campaign; however, this tends to drive down the generosity of those members able to contribute amounts greater than the average. Members with greater means need to realize that their gifts of larger amounts are needed to meet the goals. People of lesser means also need to realize that their smaller gifts are equally important to the success of the campaign.

An important benefit of the gift table is that it often provides a challenge for contributors to move their contributions into the next category. People like to feel that they are in the ranks of strong supporters of the congregation; the gift table is a means for them to measure their degree of support by comparing it to others. In soliciting gifts from potential large donors, the canvasser can use the gift table to illustrate the importance of large gifts to the campaign and to stress the opportunity the prospect has to really make a difference.

The gift table is an important element of the brochure, congregational letter, poster, and other written communication media. Like any of the messages of the campaign, its repetition in more than one media type is important. Also, the gift table is valuable information for members. It is not a substitute for relating the annual canvass to the congregational vision or mission.

The starting point in constructing a gift table is to prepare a table from the previous year's actual gifts. Using the Quartile Analysis, the weak areas of giving may be identified. Perhaps a few more large gifts are needed or a larger number of givers in the less than $500 category need to be giving in the $700 or $800 range. Another tool to use is Appendix 1: Financial Evaluation of the Congregation, which identifies the range of financial resources available. This can answer the question of the potential for larger gifts. With all of this information, a new gift table for the annual fund campaign can be generated.

5. Example of Canvass Calendar

May 21	Annual Meeting of Congregation
	New Annual Canvass Committee chair elected.
May 22-31	Members of committee recruited.
June 5	Annual Canvass Committee meets to organize.
	Plan annual canvass dates (March 17-31).
	Develop overall calendar.
	Brainstorm theme.
	Organize Communications Committee.
June 12	Communications Subcommittee meets
	Develops communication plan (to be included in overall calendar).
July 10	Communications Committee meets.
	Develops logo for canvass.
	Roughs out communications: newsletter articles, posters, mailings, brochure, Sunday announcements, personal statements of commitment.
August 7	Communications Committee meets.
	More work on communications.
September 11	Canvass Committee meets.
	Reviews communications.
	Refines overall schedule.

Plans canvasser recruitment.

Starts events planning.

October 9 Canvass Committee meets.

Reviews communications.

Reviews overall schedule.

November 13 Canvass Committee meets.

Start canvasser recruitment.

Review schedule of campaign.

December 18 Canvass Committee meets.

Review status of canvasser recruitment.

Review status of kickoff event planning.

Review status of communications.

January 10 First mailing goes out.

Letter from canvass chair announcing campaign.

January 15 Canvass Committee meets.

Review kickoff and advance gift events.

Canvasser recruitment complete.

Brochure completed.

January 28 Congregational preliminary budget meeting.

February 7 Newsletter article due.

February 8 Board approves annual canvass goal.

February 12 Canvass Committee meets.

Final planning for advance gift canvass.

Planning for kickoff event and advance gift event.

Canvasser kit completed.

February 14	Second mailing goes out.
	Brochure.
	Invitation to kickoff dinner (flyer).
February 20	Newsletter article due.
February 28	Final mailing.
	Letter from minister.
	Letter from president of congregation.
	Brochure.
February 28	Advance gift canvasser workshop held.
March 3	Coffee hour held for advance gifts members.
	Campaign chair and president speak.
March 3-10	Advance gifts canvass begins.
March 5	Newsletter article due.
March 11	Canvass Committee meets.
	Final planning for kickoff event.
	Final planning for general canvass.
March 12	Canvasser workshop held.
March 14	Canvasser workshop held.
March 16	Kickoff dinner and skit held.
	Emphasis on family.
	Announce results of advance gift canvass.
March 17	Sermon on "Giving Generously."
March 17-30	General canvass begins.
March 31	Canvass results announced.
April 1	Canvass Committee meeting.
	Follow-up plans reviewed.

April 1-15	Follow-up to canvass
	Last canvass visits made.
	Thank-you notes to contributors completed.
April 16	Thank-you letters sent to all canvass participants.
	Invitation to celebration on April 27.
April 22	Canvass Committee meeting.
	Evaluation of canvass process.
	Recommendations for next year's canvass.
	Final report on out-of-town pledges.
	Follow-up committee report.
April 27	Party for entire canvass team. CELEBRATE!!!

6. The Canvass Brochure

The canvass brochure is the single most important piece of literature in an annual canvass. It can be used multiple times as a mailing piece or insert as well as a hand-out or literature rack document.

In general, the canvass brochure should include:

1. A greeting from the minister: a simple, straightforward statement from the minister that introduces the canvass, expresses his or her feelings about what the canvass can do for the congregation as well as his or her own support, and welcomes the support of members and friends.
2. A statement on why the canvass is being conducted: a clear statement that highlights the congregation's shared vision or mission and the ministry and programs the canvass supports to move toward that vision or mission. The ministry and programs proposed are not mere daydreams but real and concrete proposals which, when accomplished, would strengthen the work of the congregation and provide meaning to the members.
3. A section on the how and when of the canvass: a brief explanation of the overall plan and organization of the canvass, the members of the Canvass Committee, the means that will be employed by the canvassers, and the calendar of events.
4. Finally, a section on how much to give, using the gift table or suggested share guide.

The most important parts of a canvass brochure are sections one and two above; they appeal to the emotions of the members and resonate with their commitment to the faith community. The greatest amount of creative effort needs to be applied to these sections to arrive at powerful yet succinct statements. Using the annual canvass theme and logo on the cover of the brochure provides a visual link to the entire communications of the canvass.

The challenge and the value of the brochure is to develop this information in a concise yet complete, attractive, and easy-to-read document. The brochure can be prepared at a reasonable cost using electronic publishing. It need not be especially elaborate; simplicity of design may make it a more effective piece. There may be someone in the congregation who has skills in designing this kind of document. A good writer along with someone with artistic talent can develop an effective brochure.

7. Congregational Assessments

Sample Congregational Assessment Form

This survey was produced by a large church in California and is an example of a fine survey. It may need modification for use in smaller congregations with 95 to 149 members.

Survey Instructions

Read over the entire survey before you answer the items. Please work independently and complete separate surveys, if more than one member of your household receives a survey.

When answering questions with a limited number of choices, please choose the answer that comes closest to the right answer for you, even if it does not fit perfectly. Unanswered items reduce the usefulness of the inventory.

Some items will require you to fill in the blanks, indicated by a blank underline. Other items, indicated by a [ ] symbol, only need a check mark. There are no absolutely "right" answers; simply do your best. There is room on the last page for your general comments or suggestions.

You need not sign your name on this questionnaire. We guarantee that your individual answers will be held in confidence.

Please return your completed survey to the church by [*date*]

Organizational Characteristics

Every congregation must deal with certain organizational concerns, such as making decisions, sharing information, and developing resources. Listed below are a number of statements describing such issues. To what extent do you believe that each statement describes your experience of our congregation?

	Strong Agreement	Moderate Agreement	Slight Disagreement	Strong Disagreement
1. I feel well informed about what the various committees and groups in the congregation are doing.	[ ]	[ ]	[ ]	[ ]
2. I see a lot of support and encouragement for trying something new in the congregation.	[ ]	[ ]	[ ]	[ ]
3. I have been encouraged to discover my gifts for ministry and service.	[ ]	[ ]	[ ]	[ ]
4. I think every member has an opportunity to hold key leadership positions.	[ ]	[ ]	[ ]	[ ]
5. I hear the religious implications of important decisions regularly discussed.	[ ]	[ ]	[ ]	[ ]
6. I am satisfied that important decisions about the congregation are usually made only after open and complete discussion by leadership and members.	[ ]	[ ]	[ ]	[ ]
7. I believe that disagreement and conflicts are dealt with openly rather than hushed up or hidden behind closed doors.	[ ]	[ ]	[ ]	[ ]
8. I find it easy to summarize for visitors and nonmembers the values, programs, and deeds behind closed doors.	[ ]	[ ]	[ ]	[ ]
9. I perceive the current morale of our members to be high and feel a sense of excitement about our congregation's future.	[ ]	[ ]	[ ]	[ ]
10. I believe that our congregation should increase or improve our outreach efforts.	[ ]	[ ]	[ ]	[ ]

Congregational Identity

Listed below are several alternatives touching upon important dimensions of any congregation's identity. Each alternative has two parts: a number scale to rate where we are and a letter scale to rate where you would like us to be.

Part 1: Using the five-point number scale between each set of alternatives, please circle the number that best describes for you where you believe our congregation currently falls. Note: "1" means most like the characteristic on the left; "3" means an equal mix of both; "5" means most like the characteristic on the right.

Part 2: Using the five-point alphabetic scale between each set of alternatives, please circle the letter that bests describes for you where you would like our congregation to be. Note: "A" means most like the characteristic on the left; "C" means an equal mix of both; "E" meaning most like the characteristic on the right.

1. Our congregation is more influenced by history and tradition.	1 A	2 B	3 C	4 D	5 E	Our congregation is more influenced by contemporary ideas and trends.
2. Our congregation is very involved with the local community.	1 A	2 B	3 C	4 D	5 E	Our congregation is not at all involved with the community around the congregation.
3. Our congregation is primarily oriented to serving our members.	1 A	2 B	3 C	4 D	5 E	Our congregation is primarily oriented to serving the world beyond our membership.
4. Our congregation feels like one large family.	1 A	2 B	3 C	4 D	5 E	Our congregation feels like a loosely knit association of individuals and groups.

5. Our congregation's approach to social issues is basically educational, leaving action up to individual conscience.	1 A	2 B	3 C	4 D	5 E	Our congregation's approach to social issues is decidedly "activist." We have a proven history of taking a stand on social issues as a congregation.
6. Our congregation's approach to the individual emphasizes education, nurturing, and gradual growth in the faith.	1 A	2 B	3 C	4 D	5 E	Our congregation's approach to the individual emphasizes the importance of the individual making a decision to make a faith commitment.
7. Our congregation gives strong expression to its denominational identity and heritage.	1 A	2 B	3 C	4 D	5 E	In our congregation it would be difficult for a visitor to know to which domination we belong.
8. Our congregation emphasizes the emotional and experiential path to spiritual growth.	1 A	2 B	3 C	4 D	5 E	Our congregation emphasizes the rational and intellectual path to spiritual growth.
9. Our congregation is too small.	1 A	2 B	3 C	4 D	5 E	Our congregation is too large.
10. Our congregation has a large degree of diversity in population characteristics and values	1 A	2 B	3 C	4 D	5 E	Our congregation has very little diversity in population characteristics and values.

Functions of the Congregation

A congregation is likely to perform a number of functions (see examples below).

List in priority order, the three functions that you think our congregation performs the best.

1. ____
2. ____
3. ____

Now list in priority order, the three functions you would emphasize for our congregation.

1. ____
2. ____
3. ____

Examples of Typical Functions

Worship services—traditional and /or contemporary

Religious education for children, youth, and/or adults

Community action on social, political, and/or economic issues

Pastoral care by visiting, counseling the sick or troubled

Social and/or fellowship opportunities

Helping members understand, deepen, and express their spiritual relationship

Supporting and sharing our values to the unchurched

Acts of charity and service for those in need

Helping members understand their use of money, time, and talents as expressions of their religion.

Tasks of the Ministers

A minister is likely to perform a number of tasks (see examples below). In your judgment what are, in priority order, the three tasks you think our ministers (collectively) perform best.

1. ______________________________

2. ______________________________

3. ______________________________

Now list in priority order the three tasks you want to be emphasized by our ministers.

1. ______________________________

2. ______________________________

3. ______________________________

Examples of Typical Ministers' Tasks

Administrative leadership

Fundraising

Planning programs and events

Membership recruitment

Presenting congregation in the community

Planning and leading worship services

Spiritual development of members

Visiting the sick, shut-ins, and the bereaved

Personal counseling of members

Religious education programs

Leadership development

Outreach/social action programs.

Our Church House

Listed below are a number of features about our facility. How would you rate them?

	Very Satisfactory	Adequate	Needs Improvement	Disaster Area
1. Is the location convenient?	[ ]	[ ]	[ ]	[ ]
2. Is the location attractive?	[ ]	[ ]	[ ]	[ ]
3. Is the landscaping attractive?	[ ]	[ ]	[ ]	[ ]
4. Are the grounds well maintained?	[ ]	[ ]	[ ]	[ ]
5. Does the building seem to need repair?	[ ]	[ ]	[ ]	[ ]
6. Is the building kept clean?	[ ]	[ ]	[ ]	[ ]
7. Do you feel safe as you attend events?	[ ]	[ ]	[ ]	[ ]
8. Are you pleased with the lighting?	[ ]	[ ]	[ ]	[ ]
9. Are you pleased with the sound quality?	[ ]	[ ]	[ ]	[ ]
10. Are you comfortable when attending events?	[ ]	[ ]	[ ]	[ ]

Qualities of a Good Worship Service

For you personally, how important are each of the following in the mix of qualities that make up a worship service.

		Essential	Important	Not Very Important	Distracting
1.	That the worship service sets forth various sides of an issue without advocating one position as the only faithful or ethical position.	[ ]	[ ]	[ ]	[ ]
2.	That the sermons express a clear, unambiguous basis of religious authority, even using illustrations from religious interpretation.	[ ]	[ ]	[ ]	[ ]
3.	That the program contains scholarly and/or literary sources of information and discusses objectively a meaningful interpretation.	[ ]	[ ]	[ ]	[ ]
4.	That the music within the service, by design, enhances and emphasizes values, emotions and/or concepts.	[ ]	[ ]	[ ]	[ ]
5.	That the worship service makes me reflect on issues and events that go beyond my personal life and local.	[ ]	[ ]	[ ]	[ ]
6.	That the worship service enhances my spiritual conviction and awareness.	[ ]	[ ]	[ ]	[ ]

Religious Attitudes

1. **Which of the following best expresses your view of human nature?**

   [ ] I believe that people are inherently good.

   [ ] I believe that people have the capacity for good and evil, but that generally good triumphs.

   [ ] I believe that people have the capacity for good and evil, but that generally evil triumphs.

   [ ] I believe that people are inherently evil.

2. **Which of the following principles most influences your life?**

   [ ] Justice, equity, and compassion in human relations and the use of democratic process.

   [ ] Respect for the interdependent web of all existence of which we are a part.

   [ ] The goal of world community with peace, liberty, and justice for all.

   [ ] The inherent worth and dignity of every person and the encouragement of one another to spiritual growth.

   [ ] A free and responsible search for truth and meaning.

3. **With which tradition do you most identify?**

   [ ] Words and deeds of prophetic women and men which challenge us to confront powers and structures of evil with justice, compassion, and the transforming power of love.

   [ ] Humanist teachings that counsel us to heed the guidance of reason and the results of science and warn us against idolatries of the mind and spirit.

   [ ] Jewish and Christian teachings that allow us to respond to God's love by loving our neighbors as ourselves.

   [ ] Direct experience of that transcending mystery and wonder, affirmed in all cultures, which moves us to a renewal of the spirit and an openness to the forces that create and uphold life.

   [ ] Wisdom from the world's religions, which inspires us in our ethical and spiritual life.

4. **Do you or your family make an annual financial pledge to the congregation?**

[ ] Yes [ ] No

If "yes," approximately how much was that pledge last year?

[ ] Under $100	[ ] $600-799	[ ] $1,500-1,999
[ ] $100-199	[ ] $800-999	[ ] $2,000-2,499
[ ] $200-399	[ ] $1,000-1,199	[ ] $2,500-3,499
[ ] $400-599	[ ] $1,200-1,499	[ ] $3,500 or more

5. **In what denomination were you raised? If you were involved with more than one denomination when you were growing up, with which one did you have the greatest identification?**

[ ] Unitarian Universalist	[ ] Roman Catholic
[ ] Protestant-Fundamentalist	[ ] Protestant-Liberal
[ ] Other Christian ____________	[ ] Jewish
[ ] Muslim	[ ] Eastern—Shinto, Hindu, Buddhist
[ ] Other ____________________	[ ] None

Background Information about Yourself

Please check [ ] all that apply

1. **Gender**

[ ] Female [ ] Male

2. **Age**

[ ] Under 19	[ ] 25-34	[ ] 45-54	[ ] 65-74
[ ] 20-24	[ ] 35-44	[ ] 55-64	[ ] 75 or over

3. **Marital Status**

[ ] Single
[ ] Widowed
[ ] Separated or divorced
[ ] Married

4. **Do you have children in any of the following age groups?**

[ ] Birth-4
[ ] 12-14
[ ] 19-22
[ ] 5-11
[ ] 15-18
[ ] Older than 22

5. **What is your highest level of formal education?**

[ ] Less than high school graduate
[ ] College degree
[ ] High school graduate
[ ] Postgraduate course work
[ ] Some college, trade or vocational school
[ ] Postgraduate degree

6. **Which of the following best describes your work relationship?**

List Occupation or Profession or Trade

Employed full-time as a: ____________________

Employed part-time as a: ____________________

Self-employed as a: ____________________

Full-time care giver for: ____________________

Looking for work usually as a: ____________________

Volunteer, full-time, as a: ____________________

Volunteer, part-time, as a: ____________________

Retired from working as a: ____________________

Student working for a degree in: ____________________

7. What is your annual household (family or single living alone) income range?

[ ] Under $10,000	[ ] $50,000-74,999
[ ] $10,000-24,999	[ ] $75,000-99,999
[ ] $25,000-49,999	[ ] $100,000 or more

8. How many years have you lived this area?

[ ] Less than 1 year	[ ] 5-9 years	[ ] 15-19 years
[ ] 1-4 years	[ ] 10-14 years	[ ] 20 years or more

9. Are you a:

[ ] Homeowner [ ] Renter [ ] Other

10. Listed below are a number of recreational activities.

Indicate your three favorite activities, beginning with the number 1.

[ ] Reading	[ ] Television	[ ] Other
[ ] Dramatic events	[ ] Sporting events	
[ ] Music	[ ] Painting/sculpture	
[ ] Hiking/nature	[ ] Crafts	
[ ] Discussion groups	[ ] Lectures	

8. The Annual Program Fund

Significant financial support for the Unitarian Universalist movement comes directly from our member congregations. Congregational contributions to the Unitarian Universalist Association Annual Program Fund (APF) provide approximately thirty-seven percent of the Association's income.

These contributions fund Association programs, services, and resources that directly benefit and strengthen the congregations themselves and Unitarian Universalism as a whole. By joining together, we can create religious education curricula and social justice programs. We can also provide support for ministry, growth, extension, and outreach. Each independent congregation has the opportunity as a group to help fund the work of the Association and to be part of an interdependent religious community.

The APF Continental Committee

The Annual Program Fund Continental Committee supports the APF campaign in the districts and works in concert with the Development Department to bring the message of Unitarian Universalist Association programs and services to congregations, encourages APF Fair Share support, and answers questions about the APF. Committee members develop strategies to enhance the Annual Program Fund through education, increased visibility, and recognition.

Members of the committee are appointed by the Board of Trustees and include a general chair; five regional chairs/liaisons; liaisons from the Unitarian Universalist Ministers Association, the Unitarian Universalist Association Board, Canadian Unitarian Council, and the District Presidents' Association; and representatives from every district of the Association. The committee meets annually in March.

Fair Share

The Fair Share is the minimum contribution your congregation is asked to give each fiscal year (July 1 to June 30). It is calculated on the basis of the number of members your congregation certified for General Assembly the previous February.

The Board of Trustees determines each year's Fair Share assessment for member congregations and the overall APF Goal. The board is guided by the Bylaws of the Association, which allow a maximum yearly increase of seven percent of the actual APF contributions in the previous fiscal year.

If your congregation's fiscal year does not coincide with the Association's and you would like assistance in budgeting for your APF contribution, please call the APF Office at 617-742-2100.

District Grants

The Association redistributes a portion of Annual Program Fund contributions to all twenty-three districts. The Annual Grant to each district is calculated in the fall of each year and paid quarterly.

The success of your Annual Program Fund campaign determines the amount of the district's grant. The more congregations give to the APF, the more is returned to your district in the form of Basic, Incentive, and Fair Share Congregation grants.

The *primary purpose* of the Unitarian Universalist Association of Congregations is to serve the needs of its member congregations, organize new congregations, extend and strengthen Unitarian Universalist institutions, and implement its Principles. *As free congregations, we enter into a covenant, promising to one another our mutual trust and support.*

For more information, contact:

Unitarian Universalist Association
Annual Program Fund Office
25 Beacon Street
Boston, MA 02108-2800
Telephone: 617-742-2100
Fax: 617-742-7025
email: idearauj@uua.org.

References

Callahan, Kennon L., *Effective Church Finances.* San Francisco: Harper San Francisco, 1992.

Callahan, Kennon L., *Giving and Stewardship in an Effective Church.* San Francisco: Harper San Francisco, 1992.

Joiner, Donald W. and Norma Wimberly, *The Abingdon Guide to Funding Ministry.* Nashville: Abingdon Press, 1995.

Needleman, Jacob, *Money and the Meaning of Life.* New York: Doubleday 1991.

Peers, Lawrence X., *The Congregational Handbook.* Boston: Unitarian Universalist Association, 1995.

Schaller, Lyle E., *44 Ways to Expand the Financial Base of Your Congregation.* Nashville: Abingdon Press, 1989.

Wilson, Marlene, *The Effective Management of Volunteer Programs.* Arlington, Virginia: VTNC, 1976.